DISCOVER
VERMONT!

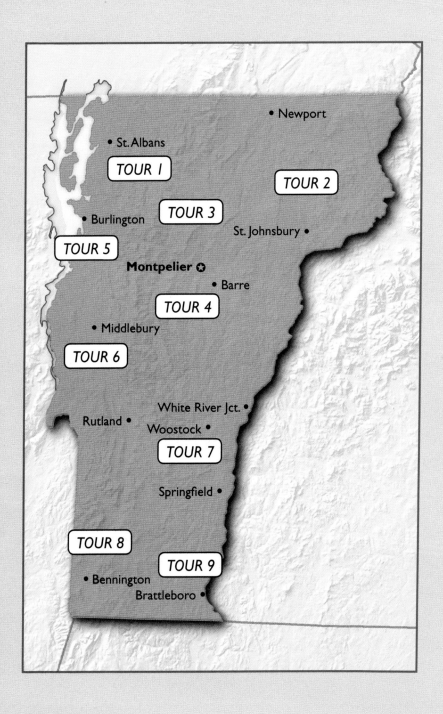

DISCOVER VERMONT!

The *Vermont Life* Guide to Exploring Our Rural Landscape

Mark Bushnell

Jointly published by
Vermont Life Magazine
Montpelier, Vermont,
and
Billings Farm & Museum
Woodstock, Vermont,
with
additional support from
Cabot Creamery Cooperative
Cabot, Vermont

First edition

PHOTO LIST
Tour 1, page 15: Grand Isle landscape. (Courtesy Special Collections, University
of Vermont)
Tour 2, page 39: Gathering sap in the Northeast Kingdom. (Courtesy Special
Collections, University of Vermont)
Tour 3, page 57: Horse-drawn wagon hauling milk containers at original Cabot
creamery in Cabot, circa 1919. (Courtesy Cabot Creamery Cooperative)
Tour 4, page 75: Farm and household staff of the Moulton Bros. Green Mountain
Stock Farm in Randolph, circa 1885. (From *Early Photographs of Randolph
Vermont 1855-1948* by Wes Herwig. Greenhills Books, Randolph Center,
Vermont, 1986)
Tour 5, page 91: Shelburne Farms farm barn. (Courtesy Special Collections,
University of Vermont)
Tour 6, page 109: Sheep farming in Vermont. (Courtesy Vermont Historical
Society)
Tour 7, page 125: Billings Farm, 1950s. (Courtesy Billings Family Archives)
Tour 8, page 143: Milking scene postcard. (Courtesy Vermont Historical Society)
Tour 9, page 155:Farm family in haywagon. (Courtesy Vermont Historical Society)

Edited and produced by Julie Stillman
Cover and interior design by Faith Hague
Cover photo by Alan L. Graham
Maps by David J. Goodman

Library of Congress Cataloging-in-Publication Data:

Bushnell, Mark, 1964-
Discover Vermont! : the Vermont Life guide to exploring our rural landscape /
Mark Bushnell. — 1st ed.
p. cm.
Includes index.
ISBN 1-931389-14-4 (pbk.)
1. Vermont—Guidebooks I. Title.
F47.3.B875 2005
917.4304'44—dc22   2005006378

Printed in the United States of America

ACKNOWLEDGMENTS

This book is the product of a working partnership between *Vermont Life* Magazine, Billings Farm & Museum, and Cabot Creamery Cooperative. All three partners contributed their expertise and financial support to this project. The book also received financial support from the Vermont Department of Tourism & Marketing, for which the publishers are grateful.

The partners also wish to acknowledge the work and expertise of author Mark Bushnell, book packager Julie Stillman, and designer Faith Hague. Thanks to Beth Kennett of Vermont Farms! and Liberty Hill Farm for her expert advice and for the blueberry cake. Thanks to Paul Carnahan at the Vermont Historical Society and Prudence Doherty at the Special Collections Library at the University of Vermont for assistance with photo research.

A special thanks to David Donath, President of The Woodstock Foundation, for the original concept of the book, and for counsel and advice as the project took form.

The partners especially wish to acknowledge and thank the farmers, farm families, and foresters of Vermont, whose labors have created and maintained the beauty of the Vermont landscape.

CONTENTS

INTRODUCTION

Farming has shaped Vermont.

It is what first brought people to settle the state, why others have followed, and why so many have stayed. It is also probably, whether you realize it or not, at least part of the reason you are here. And that might be because of the state's beauty and its reputation for unspoiled countryside. This book will help you explore how agriculture has affected the look of the landscape you will see, the feel of the villages you will visit, the character of the people you will meet.

Vermont is unique because farming remains a dominant presence here even as it has lost its central role elsewhere in New England. Southern New England feels different from Vermont because it is far more densely populated and developed. And although the rest of northern New England shares some of Vermont's rural nature, neither Maine nor New Hampshire is widely farmed.

So what difference exactly does farming make? Most obvious is the way it makes a place look. Much of Vermont's land remains open because of working farms. If it weren't for agriculture—particularly forms of animal farming, such as dairying—the state would revert to the heavily forested landscape Europeans first encountered when they settled here. Forests are beautiful and natural, but a vista that is not punctuated by farms lacks the human touch, the reminder of how we are connected to the land.

Farming gave us not only fields, but also villages. As people moved into Vermont, they cleared large tracts of land to cultivate crops and raise livestock. At the center of a cluster of farms, a village would form and exert a gravitational pull that helped bind the community. Here a few businesses—perhaps a blacksmith or a general store—might spring up to serve the farms. And here you would find the town meeting hall, where farmers and other residents would gather to govern themselves.

Town meeting is an ideal form of government for farmers, since everybody gets his or her say. Farmers would have it no other way. Working the land and controlling their own destinies gives farmers a sense of self-respect, a sense that their opinions matter as much as the rich man's down the road.

Over the years, farmers have imbued the state with this belief. Vermont today still thinks of itself as an egalitarian society. That sense of equality, and the state's small size, help us view our political leaders as peers, not superiors. We are more likely to call our recent governors by their first names—Madeleine, Howard, or Jim—than by their title. And we are one of the few states that never felt it was appropriate to build a governor's mansion.

We've learned from farmers that we don't need to show deference to show respect. We've also learned that the best way to earn respect is to work hard. It is a lesson straight off the farm, where goofing off can have dire consequences. Farmers have an old expression, "Push the work; don't let it push you," and other Vermonters have taken it to heart.

If Vermonters have learned to show deference for anything, it is nature. Farmers have learned the hard way—through trial and error—what and where nature will let you farm in Vermont. Succeeding waves of settlers cleared land to make room for their farmsteads, and they have logged to reap the value of the timber. Gradually, as the best land was claimed, newer arrivals began to clear the mountainsides for farmland. The effect was disastrous. At one point, the state was 80 percent cleared—hardly recognizable to a Vermonter today. The harmful effects went beyond aesthetics. Damage was done to the soil at higher elevations, which was already thin when the axes began to swing. Stripped of its trees, the soil eroded. Farmers then moved on to continue the sad cycle by clearing more sloping land.

Eventually, economics caught up with farmers working marginal lands and their farms slowly returned to forest. Today the relationship between forest and farmland has been reversed and 80 percent of the state is now wooded.

Vermont's concern about agriculture is no longer over-farming; it is keeping the farms we've got. Over the years, the state's farms have had to evolve to stay profitable. Long gone are the days when the Champlain Valley was known as New England's breadbasket because of all the wheat it grew, and when sheep outnumbered cows and people.

The current generation of Vermonters is exploring an amazing array of ways to keep the land in use. Most of that worked land remains in dairy farming. This traditional form of farming, which has long been the backbone of Vermont's agricultural economy, is changing. The most obvious way is in sheer numbers. The state has fewer than 1,500 dairy farms, where a little more than half a century ago it had more than 11,000. Despite the consolidation, dairying remains largely a family operation. The average Vermont farm today milks 100 cows, hardly a mega-farm. Dairy farmers have improved breeds and introduced other technologies to greatly boost milk output. The last half-century has seen the number of dairy cows in Vermont almost cut in half, but the total amount of milk produced nearly double.

Farming is rapidly changing across Vermont. Some dairy farmers are going organic out of social concern and for the higher prices their products bring. Other farmers are trying different crops, animals, and products for new markets. Sheep farming, which once dominated the state, is experiencing a resurgence; exotic animals, such as llama, alpaca, and emu, are arriving and creating a new niche; new cheesemakers are setting up shop and adding to Vermont's already strong reputation as a source of great cheese; and some farmers and entrepreneurs are finding a valuable new crop, grapes, for the state's nascent wine industry. In addition to marketing this wide variety of products in-state and beyond, some farms are open to visitors and sell their products on-site as well.

Other changes are not as visible but are just as real. Nonprofit land trusts are working with farmers to buy their development rights, giving farmers much-needed income and forever preserving portions of the state as farmland.

Vermonters are also reaffirming the connection between farms and food. Today Vermont is very much a food state. If such things were measured, we would no doubt be near the top of the list of bread makers per capita—or, for that matter, beer brewers or cheese-makers or growers of organic produce per capita. We may be small, but we are diverse, and we take our food seriously.

This book is intended to introduce you to Vermont's working landscape through a series of driving tours. Each of these nine "agri-tourism" excursions is intended to highlight the types of farms the state has to offer, as well as some museums dedicated to telling the story of Vermont agriculture. You can follow a tour through the rich Valley of Vermont in the southwest or the traditional dairy country of the northwest; through the rich farming heritage of the east-central part of the state to the new cheesemaking region developing in the southeast.

As you tour Vermont, you'll see the diversity and how disparate businesses work together, whether it is at a farm-operated shop or farm stand, a local farmers' market, or at one of the many restaurants that make a point of serving Vermont produce and meats. Most of all, you will see that without farming Vermont wouldn't be Vermont.

∾ How to Use This Book

This book will take you on nine tours through Vermont's rural land-scape. This type of travel has been dubbed "agritourism." One farmer who long ago opened his farm to the public prefers to em-phasize the fun you'll have along the way, so he coined the phrase "agritainment."

Don't be fooled by the driving times listed at the top of each route. These are estimates only, and are there just to give you an idea of how much time you will spend in your car. The driving time estimates assume an average speed between 30 and 40 miles per hour. Most of the tours would take you only a few hours to navigate. But you will want to get out of your car and explore the sights along the way, so a tour that takes only, say, three hours to drive, might actually take you two or three days to complete. It all depends on how much time you have, and what strikes your fancy.

The tours are full of interesting sights, places we are confident that many people will enjoy. This book, however, is not intended to be encyclopedic. We know there are many entertaining and engaging places we couldn't include because they were off the routes we created, or because we just didn't have room for everything. In some cases we wanted to suggest sites that just didn't fit geographically into one of the tours. We have included some of these as side trips, so you can visit them if they pique your interest.

You will want to have a state highway map with you as you drive. If you are a regular visitor to Vermont (or plan to become one), you might want to purchase the *Vermont Atlas & Gazetteer*, published by DeLorme, or the *Vermont Road Atlas & Guide*, published by Northern Cartographic—they provide detailed maps of the state, including back roads.

So use this book as just what it is—a guide. Travel a whole route, or just part of one, and follow your nose. If you go off exploring, you might just find a treasure we missed.

Each tour follows a suggested order in which to visit places. You can, of course, join the route at any place along the loop, skip parts, or add others. For your convenience, we have also recommended places to eat, places to stay, and ways to find other accommodations. Where possible, the lodgings are tied to working farms and are always within an agricultural area. Almost all of the restaurants listed are members of the Vermont Fresh Network, whose members are

Helpful Web Sites

Check out the state's official travel page, the most comprehensive listing of lodgings, restaurants, events and more: www.vermontvacation.com

Connect to working farms that offer overnight accommodations or buy products directly from working farms: www.vermontfarms.org

Learn about Vermont's growing cheese industry and discover which companies are open for visits: www.vtcheese.com

Learn the history of Vermont's apple industry and where to find dozens of varieties today: www.vermontapples.org

Discover where to buy a Vermont Christmas tree: www.vermontagriculture.com/ctindex.htm

Locate a sugarhouse that is open to the public or order some maple products: www.vermontmaple.org

Learn details about and links to the state's specialty foods makers: www.vermontspecialtyfoods.org

Learn about the state's dairy farms and the food they make: www.vermontdairy.com

Connect to the state's many beer brewers, winemakers, cideries, and brewpubs: www.vermontbrewers.com

Find restaurants that team up with local farms to provide Vermont-grown and produced food: www.vermontfresh.net

committed to serving local fresh ingredients. At the end of each tour, we have included telephone numbers and Web addresses to help you plan your trip. Other, more general Web sites are listed above.

Enjoy yourself as you explore Vermont's rural landscape.

Northwestern Vermont

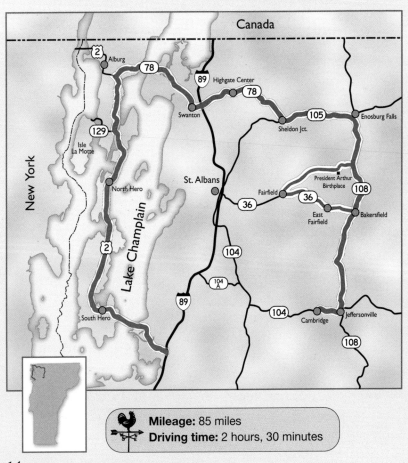

Canada

New York

Alburg

78

89 Highgate Center

78

2

129

Isle
La Motte

Swanton

105

Enosburg Falls

Sheldon Jct.

North Hero

St. Albans

Fairfield

President Arthur
Birthplace

108

Lake Champlain

36

36

East
Fairfield

Bakersfield

104

2

104
A

89

South Hero

104

Cambridge

Jeffersonville

108

Mileage: 85 miles
Driving time: 2 hours, 30 minutes

Land of Wine, Cheese, Milk, and Apples

Driving through northwestern Vermont, you will pass through a world of contrasts. It is a deeply traditional place populated by people who have farmed the same land for generations. It is also a place where old families and new arrivals are finding innovative ways to work the land, and a place that welcomes people who are just passing through to enjoy the spectacular scenery.

That scenery itself is diverse. The eastern and southern parts of the region are full of rich farm valleys that look out on some of the tallest peaks in the Green Mountains. Head north and west however, and you'll soon find yourself among farms that squeeze onto rolling fields surrounded by hills. Then, gradually, those hills give way and you are in the northern end of the Champlain Valley, a wide, flat, fertile expanse of land that is ideal for farming.

The farms extend all the way to the edge of Lake Champlain. And across a slender ribbon of the lake, you will find islands on which dairy farms still operate. But here they are joined by long-standing orchards that take advantage of the warming lake effect, as well as by agriculturalists who are raising beef cattle or demonstrating the area's suitability as a wine region.

This tour will take us from the town of Cambridge, with its fertile farmland that sits astride the Lamoille River, to Jeffersonville, which sits at the base of the Green Mountains and is part ski town, part traditional community. From there, we will travel north into Franklin County, which is one of the most intensely agricultural parts of the state. Then we will head west to the Lake Champlain Islands, which have a mix of year-round residents and seasonal home-owners. Farming remains part of the culture. Here, fruit farming dominates, with long-established orchards operating near a new vineyard that is helping establish Vermont as a winemaking area.

➻ Cambridge and Jeffersonville

The first stops on this tour are in Cambridge and Jeffersonville, where you'll visit a winery and a maple syrup maker. To reach Cambridge, take Route 108 from Stowe over the mountains, then Route 15 West from Jeffersonville; or take Route 15 East from the Burlington area; or take Interstate 89 to Exit 18, then get on Route 104A East and follow it to Route 104 East.

Our first stop, the Boyden Valley Winery, is located west of the center of Cambridge, at the junction of Routes 104 and 15.

Boyden Valley Winery
The two worlds that northwestern Vermont represents collide on the

Boyden family's farm. For the past four generations, spanning a century, Boydens have worked the 100-acre farm that anchors the west end of the town of Cambridge. The farm is situated in the Lamoille River Valley, which is hemmed in by hills to the north and south and by the Green Mountains to the east. Like most Vermont farmers, the Boydens had dairy cows and made maple syrup each spring and cider each fall.

About a decade ago, David Boyden, who was then in his late twenties, had an idea: why not start a vineyard? It was an odd notion. Vermont's climate is seldom confused with California's. Besides, what did the Boydens know about making wine? But David Boyden was fascinated by winemaking and wanted to turn what was a hobby into a profession. He planted grapes on six sloping acres that had never been much good for growing anything. To probably everyone's surprise but his own, the vineyard now produces some excellent grapes and Boyden Valley Winery is now on the map.

Boyden and his wife, Linda, have restored and converted an old 1878 carriage barn. They use the downstairs to make thirteen different varieties of wine. The upstairs has been turned into a nicely appointed tasting room and retail shop. Boyden has won international awards for his wine, but he is constantly using his experience to improve his wines and to find new, hardier grape varieties to grow.

In addition to its five grape wines, Boyden Valley makes wines from many other fruits as well: apples, blueberries, cranberries (purchased from the state's only bog in nearby Fletcher), pears, and rhubarb. The Boydens are particularly proud of their dessert wines—Gold Leaf, which combines an apple wine with hints of maple syrup; and their new Cassis, a wine made from currants.

Milk House Market

Another branch of the Boyden family has launched an unconventional farm-based business. David Boyden's sister-in-law, Lauri, runs the Milk House Market. As the name suggests, the store is located in the farm's former milk house, which is beside the barn where her husband, Mark, used to raise dairy cows.

Today the market sells the hormone-free beef and pork that Mark now raises. The Boydens also stock lamb, turkey, and chicken raised on area farms, as well as local produce. Lauri says she is glad she is able to provide area farmers a market for their goods. While the store has become something of a local market, Lauri hopes to attract visitors and their children who want to spend time on a farm. So, in addition to enticing people with local honey, salsas, farm-fresh eggs, Vermont cheeses, and gifts and kitchen items for the home, the Milk House Market also features a 12-acre corn maze, a petting zoo, and a summer ice cream shop.

Vermont Maple Outlet

Next we'll head to Jeffersonville to visit an agricultural operation that is updating a Vermont tradition. To get to the Vermont Maple Outlet, head east on Route 15, through the town of Cambridge, where Vermont's tallest mountain, 4,393-foot-high Mount Mansfield, provides a dramatic backdrop. Two miles east of Cambridge, you'll come to the Vermont Maple Outlet.

This is the retail end of an efficient, modern operation owned by the Marsh family, who have modernized over the eighty-five-plus years they have been making maple syrup. Most people think of maple sugaring as an old-fashioned business. Perhaps the idea conjures up images of a horse—or, if the image is more modern, a tractor—pulling a sleigh topped by a large tank that holds all the sap farmers find as they check the buckets hanging from trees every year in early spring.

Today most large-scale maple sugar makers rely on much more up-to-date technology. Visiting the Vermont Maple Outlet will quickly teach you how far maple sugaring has evolved. Maple products and other Vermont goods take up most of the public space at the outlet, but the Marshes have set up a one-room exhibit to explain the innovations in maple sugaring. The displays demonstrate how some sugarers began moving away from metal sap buckets in the 1940s (although most smaller operations, and some larger ones, still use them). Replacing the buckets were rudimentary tin tubing systems, which were attached to taps on the trees. Today, tin is out and flexible plastic tubing systems are widely used instead.

The industry has also moved toward using smaller-diameter spouts that are easier on the trees. The result, the exhibit explains, is healthier trees that live longer and produce more sap, which is what any maple sugarer would want.

The outlet also includes a small store, featuring maple syrup and candies, t-shirts, postcards, and knickknacks.

✦ Franklin County

Next, we'll take a drive north into Franklin County, the state's most traditional farming community. Here, dairy is still king and the area looks much as it did 30 years ago. From the maple outlet we'll continue east on Route 15 for 1 mile and then turn left onto Route 108 North.

The road passes through some lovely countryside. We'll travel 18 miles to reach the heart of this dairy country. This is a rolling, bucolic ride. Along the way, you'll see llama farms and tree farms and, of course, more conventional dairy farms. If you want to make a side trip, see page 20 for a suggested route. The tour, however, is continuing north to the region's bastion of dairying, Enosburg.

✦ Enosburg Falls

As you approach Enosburg, you know you are in serious dairy country by the farms that ring the town—you might even note that some of the green street signs bear little white cows on them. Enosburg

 **Side Trip**

Fairfield and the
Chester Arthur Homestead

If you want to explore a bit on your own before you get as far north as Enosburg, you can make a side trip that will take you through one of Vermont's great farming towns and to a presidential birthplace. To get there from Jeffersonville drive north on Route 108 for 10 miles until you meet up with Route 36 in Bakersfield. Turn left on Route 36 West. The road will take you to the lovely community of Fairfield, where most people still live on farms.

Turn right at Fairfield's four corners, which will bring you onto South Road. (Immediately on your right after turning, you will see Chester's on the Square, a tiny restaurant that is a favorite among local farmers. If it is lunchtime, ask the staff to make you a sandwich or dish up one of their salads. The food is hearty, the portions large, and the prices more than reasonable. You'll want to save room for dessert. Chester's is known for its cookies, pies, and other sweets.)

Continue on South Road and then take your first right onto Chester Arthur Road. After about 5 miles you'll come to the childhood homestead of the former president, and Fairfield's favorite son.

Arthur is little remembered, probably because his main initiatives—involving civil service and tariff code reform—are hardly the stuff of legend. At the site, you will find a re-creation of the simple home Arthur moved into in 1830 or '31, when he was a one-year-old.

Arthur was born nearby. Exactly where was hotly debated during his political career. His rivals claim he was born just over the Canadian border, in Dunham, Quebec, making him ineligible to be president—and some evidence supports their claims. The homestead contains an exhibit on Arthur's life and career.

To return to the tour, continue down Chester Arthur Road, and you will meet up with Route 108 again in 2 miles. Turn left onto Route 108 North.

is the kind of town where you'll see an occasional tractor rumble through downtown and where the biggest event of the year is the Dairy Festival held for four days each year at the beginning of June.

Route 108 will bring you to the edge of the village of Enosburg Falls. You will pass the junction with Route 105. Drive a couple of blocks and park if you would like to explore. To continue the tour, turn onto Route 105 and follow it west.

None of the farms in the immediate area is open regularly to the public. It is almost as if people here are so familiar with farming that they have trouble imagining that other people have anything to learn about it.

But since we *are* in dairy country, we will visit two dairy farms nearby in Highgate Center and Swanton.

↯ Highgate and Swanton

As we head west from Enosburg the view is farm after farm after farm. Route 105 passes by cornfields and cupola-topped barns along a broad, flat valley that borders the Missisquoi River.

Also roughly following the road is a 26-mile-long bike path linking St. Albans City and Richford on the Canadian border. Both communities thrived during the heyday of the railroads. St. Albans, whose nickname is the Rail City, now has a more diversified industrial base and has a pleasant downtown. The city, which is ringed by farms, is the largest community in Franklin County. At the other end of the line, Richford still has the imposing public buildings of a once-prosperous town, but it struggled as railroad traffic slowed during the second half of the twentieth century. Efforts are now under way to revitalize the town.

You will follow Route 105 for 7 miles before you see Route 78 on your right. Turn onto Route 78 heading west. Over the next 6 miles, the road will take you through the small cluster of houses known as Shawville and then through East Highgate before bringing you into Highgate Center.

Here we'll turn right onto Route 207 North. Our destination, Green Mountain Blue Cheese, is 2.5 miles down the road. The farm is on the left and marked with the sign Boucher Family Farm. The barn and cheesemaking area are set back from the road.

Other Vermont Cheesemakers

Vermont cheesemakers used to be known for one thing: Cheddahhh! But the field has become much more diverse recently. Heck, even long-time cheddar makers are branching out.

Today the state is full of cheesemakers who are producing some of the world's best cheeses. That's no empty boast. They have the national and international awards to back it up. Among these award winners are relatively new cheesemakers who are winning a loyal following by getting back to basics, using Old World techniques. Many of the cheeses they make are classified as "farmstead" (meaning they are made from milk produced on the cheesemaker's farm) and/or "artisanal" (meaning they are made by hand, not with machines).

Among the farms earning Vermont a reputation for producing fine cheeses are:

Major Farm, Westminster West

Cindy and David Major make a revered farmhouse sheep cheese. Their signature cheese, Vermont Shepherd, is made from raw sheep's milk in a style they studied in the French Pyrenees. They also make two cows' milk cheeses, Putney Tomme, a tangy farmhouse cheese; and Timson, a soft creamy variety. The Majors have served as mentors to aspiring cheesemakers interested in joining the state's burgeoning ranks.

Green Mountain Blue Cheese

Dawn Morin-Boucher married into a dairying family. Her husband, whose family moved to Vermont from Canada in the 1920s, can trace his farming roots back eleven generations. One day at the Boucher breakfast table the family was debating how to make the farm more profitable. The idea of increasing the size of their herd was raised and rejected. Then Dawn suggested she could begin using some of the farm's milk to make cheese.

Thus Green Mountain Blue Cheese was born. With a great deal

Woodcock Farm, Weston

Mark and Gari Fischer studied cheesemaking with the Majors. When they started producing cheese, it was aged in the Majors' cave and marketed under the Vermont Shepherd label. Now Woodcock Farm sells its sheep cheeses under its own label. Offerings include Weston Wheel, which has a distinctive bite with lingering sweet nutty flavors; Summer Snow, a creamy cheese with hints of mushroom and lemon flavors; and West River Feta, a tangy cheese made in a Bulgarian style.

Lazy Lady Farm, Westfield

The real lazy ladies on this farm are the goats, jokes cheesemaker Laini Fondiller, who says she pampers her animals. She makes great organic cheese, which she sells at the Montpelier Farmers' Market on Saturdays in season and at select food stores.

You can visit these and other cheesemakers online at www.vtcheese.com, the Web site of the Vermont Cheese Council. Links on the page will direct you to the Vermont Cheese Trail, which offers detailed information. If you are interested in visiting cheesemakers, check the cheese council's Web page to see which ones are open for visits.

of trial and error, Dawn figured out what type of cheese she would make and the best way to go about it. Her hard work has paid off: Since 1999 her cheese has been winning awards, and more important, loyal customers. She now makes three kinds: Vermont Blue Cheese; an Italian blue named Gore-Dawn-Zola; and Brother Laurent, a cross between a St. Paulin and Livarot, which she named after her husband's uncle.

Dawn makes cheese one or two days a week, pumping the milk fresh and warm straight from the cows in the milking parlor into the cheesemaking room. Since this is a working farm, someone is usually around to answer your questions. If no one is there, Dawn leaves samples of her cheeses in the refrigerator, where you'll also find wedges you can buy.

Carman Brook Maple & Dairy Farm

Karen and Daniel Fortin went another direction with their dairy farm, located in Swanton. Instead of making cheese, they invite visitors to stop by the farm to explore both their dairying and their maple sugaring operations.

To get to the Fortins' place from the Boucher farm, return to Highgate Center and look for the junction of Routes 207 and 78. Turn right onto Route 78 West. Follow this road for 3.4 miles until you see Frontage Road on your right. Turn onto Frontage Road. When you reach a stop sign after 3.5 miles, continue straight. This stretch is called Fortin Road. The farm is 1 mile ahead on your left.

Daniel and Karen Fortin had been dairying for years when they decided to begin making maple syrup at their farm, which had been in Daniel's family since 1911. So in 1999 they built a sugarhouse and opened it to the public.

The Carman Brook Farm is open to the public Tuesday through Saturday from March to mid-November. If you are visiting between Memorial Day and Labor Day, get there at 10 a.m. for Karen's guided tour. Otherwise, you are welcome to take the self-guided tour through the sugarhouse and cow barn. You can also take a walk through the sugar woods and explore caves that were used by Native Americans into the early twentieth century. If that sounds like too much work, you can relax at one of the picnic tables or meet the animals at the petting zoo. The Fortins invite you to linger at their farm. In fact, they have stocked their sugarhouse with farm-related books and puzzles for visitors to use.

From here, we'll head to Alburg and the Champlain Islands, with a stop at an orchard in West Swanton. Return down Frontage Road to Route 78, turn right, and follow the road west into downtown Swanton. The road curves around the village green and then crosses the Missisquoi River and heads north out of town. Route 78 follows the river for several miles. You will be driving through the Missisquoi National Wildlife Refuge, a great spot to see heron, osprey, and waterfowl. When the river bends away to your right, you will be on Hog Island, a chunk of land connected to the mainland by this causeway. Long ago, farmers used to bring their hogs over by boat for the summer and let them forage for acorns before rounding them up for slaughter.

West Swanton Orchards

A couple miles outside downtown Swanton on Route 78 you will see West Swanton Orchards, Farm Market, and Cider Mill on your right. The orchard store is open each May through December, selling apples (in season), cider, pies, doughnuts, and souvenirs. In the fall the orchard is open for pick-your-own apples. The orchard, which you can tour, covers 62 acres and produces 11 varieties of apples.

↝ Alburg

From West Swanton, Route 78 will cross the Missisquoi Bay Bridge to Alburg. You will feel like you are heading onto the islands, but Alburg is really a spit of land that divides the northern end of the lake, separating the Missisquoi Bay and the Richelieu River. Although it has the feel of an island—you can see the lake from most of the roads—dairy farming remains economically important to the area.

Lakeside Berry Farm

Just 1.5 miles after crossing the bridge to East Alburg on Route 78 you'll come to another fruit farm. Nancy and Ed Christopher's berry farm is open from August through about mid-October for pick-your-own raspberries. At their farm stand they also sell vegetables, blackberries, and blueberries grown on nearby farms.

Nancy Christopher knows the land well, having grown up here back when the farm was a dairy operation. Her grandfather originally leased the land. Her father later bought it and ran the farm as a dairy for fifty-seven years. After the family sold the herd in 1993, the Christophers started growing raspberries. They now have 8 or 9 acres in raspberries and lease the other roughly 67 acres to an organic farmer who grows hay.

Before we leave Alburg, let's visit a farmer who is making cow and goat cheese by the water's edge.

Lakes End Cheeses

Lakes End Cheeses is located on West Shore Road in Alburg. To get there from the berry farm, continue west on Route 78 until it meets Route 2. Cross Route 2 and follow the truck route 1.8 miles to West Shore Road. Turn left and after just under a mile you'll see Lakes End Cheeses on your left.

Joanne James moved to Vermont to live with her husband, Alton, on the land he grew up on, and began making cheese. Their small farm has a striking view of the lake. There they raise ten goats and four cows, which produce enough milk for her cheesemaking operation. Joanne has experimented and now uses varying amounts of the two types of milk to make her six cheeses.

She started by making just Misty Cove Pure and Misty Cove Blended. Pure is made with straight cow's milk, producing a firm, sharp cheese, with a sweet taste. For Blended, she used some goat's milk to add a tangy aftertaste. In addition, she now makes Champlain Chevre, James Bay, Harbor Light, and Samuel D's Soft. Joanne makes cheese four days a week, so if you are lucky you might get to watch her in action. Call ahead to arrange a tour.

Before she took on cheesemaking, Joanne's business was making chocolates. Her Shoreline Chocolates are sold only by mail order or at the farm, which has a gift shop that also carries her cheeses. If your visit doesn't coincide with business hours, the farm has an outdoor cooler stocked with the cheeses that she operates on the honor system.

❧ The Champlain Islands

From Lakes End Cheeses, we will drive on to the Lake Champlain Islands. Turn left onto West Shore Road and follow it 2.4 miles to Route 129. The tour heads east; to the west is Isle La Motte, which has a written history dating back to early colonial times. It is also home to the world's oldest fossil reef (see Side Trip, page 28). Turn left and follow Route 129 East for 2.8 miles, to its end at Route 2. Turn right onto Route 2 East, where you will cross the bridge to North Hero island. We will be heading south to South Hero.

Farming is mostly on the wane in the islands as the farmland has been sold to build homes. But agricultural pursuits still continue on a handful of surviving dairy farms, on apple orchards, and on a vineyard. As you drive south, you'll see reminders of the islands' former glory as fertile ground for agriculture. Every once in a while along the road, you'll see a sizable old stone house. These homes are remnants from the 1820s, when the opening of the Champlain Canal between the lake and the Hudson River created a massive new market—New York City—for Champlain Valley farmers. In just a few years, farmers became rich selling wheat to the city, and some of them showed off their new wealth by building these stately homes. The boom was short-lived, however, as the completion of the Erie Canal, connecting western New York State farmers with the city, gave Vermonters some stiff competition.

 Side Trip

Isle La Motte Fossil Reef

Lake Champlain certainly has a look of permanence. In truth, the lake as we know it has been around a scant 20,000 years, a blink of an eye in geological terms. To give you a sense of how relatively young that is, check out the Chazy fossil reef on Isle La Motte.

The reef is believed to be the oldest in the world. It formed roughly 480 million years ago, at a time when most of the land that is now Vermont was located roughly 30 degrees south of the equator. The ancient continent Laurentia, which contained the reef, shifted north and its crust was forced under an equally ancient ocean. The shift brought Vermont toward its current position (and the collision created the Green Mountains).

The best place to see the reef is at the old Fisk Quarry on the west shore of Isle La Motte. To reach the preserved 24-acre site, which is well interpreted with signs, from Lakes End Cheeses turn left onto West Shore Road and follow it 2.4 miles to Route 129. Turn right onto Route 129, which will take you onto Isle La Motte. After 1 mile, turn right onto Shrine Road. Follow it for less than 1 mile, then turn left at the lakeshore onto West Shore Road.

Almost immediately you will pass by Saint Anne's Shrine, which marks the spot where in 1666 the first Catholic mass was said in what would become Vermont. The road follows the shoreline and offers wonderful views of the lake. After about 4 miles, you will pass the Fisk Farm on your left, immediately followed by the Fisk Quarry and its small parking area.

Walking, hiking, snowshoeing, and cross-country skiing are permitted at the site, which is open dawn to dusk.

Still, produce from Vermont farms continued to flow south. Later in the nineteenth century, apples from the islands were a major export. Then, during World War II, Grand Isle County yellow beans left the state by the boxcar to help the war effort.

↩ North Hero and South Hero

Today you'll see farming as you drive through the Champlain Islands, but of a less intensive sort. Route 2 will carry you south through North Hero and on to South Hero, which are commonly thought to have been named after Vermont patriots Ethan Allen of Fort Ticonderoga fame and his brother, Ira. The Allens are widely considered the state's main founders. Historians believe, however, that the heroes being commemorated were all of America's Revolutionary War veterans, not just the Allens.

The road through the islands stays mostly to their east side, so the views tend to be across the lake to the Green Mountains. Occasionally the islands narrow enough that you can catch a glimpse of New York's Adirondack Mountains to the southwest. One particularly narrow spot in North Hero, which you will reach about 4 miles after crossing the bridge from Alburg, is called the Carrying Place, because Native Americans used to carry their canoes overland here rather than paddling either north or south around the island. Settlers later learned of the shortcut, which was especially popular among smugglers during the early nineteenth century.

Hero's Welcome
A mile south of the Carrying Place, you will come to the small village of North Hero and its outsized store, Hero's Welcome. The business is one of those stores where you can find seemingly anything. The store carries fine wines and gourmet foods, videos, sweatshirts, pottery, kitchenware, books, artwork, and outdoor furniture.

It also makes sandwiches that bear the names of local Revolutionary War heroes and others, as well as soups and pizza. If you get there early, you can pick up some breakfast pastries. Across the street, the store has set up picnic tables beside the lake with great views toward Vermont's Green Mountains.

After going another 3 miles south on Route 2 you will reach a drawbridge that will carry you over to South Hero island, the northern part of which is the town of Grand Isle.

Eight miles south of the drawbridge, at the blinking light in South Hero you will see a sign for Route 314 (don't turn at the first sign in Grand Isle). Turn right and follow Route 314 West. After .6 mile, turn left onto Eagle Camp Road. When it dead-ends into West Shore Road, turn left. As you follow West Shore Road south, you will pass several bays that offer wonderful views of the broad lake. Keep going for about 3 miles until you see Snow Farm Vineyard on your left.

Snow Farm Vineyard

The idea of creating a vineyard and winery in Vermont started a decade ago when a couple was having a conversation over glasses of — what else? — wine. Harrison and Molly Lebowitz were bemoaning the fate of agriculture in the state. Their neighbors in the town of Georgia had just gone bankrupt and had had to sell their farm. Wasn't there some new way to use farmland so that agriculture could be profitable? Harrison asked. As he spoke he looked at the wine bottle and wondered why there weren't any vineyards in Vermont.

From that moment, Snow Farm Vineyard was born. At the time, Harrison was working as a lawyer for the Vermont attorney general's office. He used his spare time to research winemaking and possible vineyard sites around the state. He found what he was looking for on South Hero, which has a milder climate than most of Vermont because the island is surrounded by Lake Champlain. So he quit his job with the state and became a vintner.

With the help of investors, the Lebowitzes bought 20 acres near the lakeshore and began planting grapes. The center of the operation is a barnlike building that sits beside the road. That's where they put the tasting room, winemaking room, and office.

Snow Farm now produces wines from its own grapes. The flavors aim at a variety of palates, ranging from sweet to tart. To make wine in Vermont, you have to know more grape varieties than Chardonnay, Riesling, and Merlot. You have to be familiar with uncommon types, too, such as Baco Noir, Seyval Blanc, and Cayuga, all of which Snow Farm has had success growing.

Harrison hopes that the vineyard will inspire other Vermonters to try this new crop. He is optimistic that the operation will prove profitable enough for them to keep their land in agriculture, rather than sell it for development. Eventually, he envisions Vermont becoming a popular winemaking region rivaling other cold weather locales such as New York State, Oregon, and Ontario. He is not alone in his dream, as the presence of Boyden Valley Winery and others in Vermont makes clear.

Snow Farm also stocks wine-related gifts and Vermont cheeses and other foods—just the right items to put together a picnic. And, speaking of picnics, you'll want to bring one to Snow Farm if you happen to be there on a Thursday night in the summertime: the vineyard offers a free concert series and opens the tasting room in case you want to buy a bottle to enjoy along with your picnic.

By the way, if you are a bicycling enthusiast, consider a ride through the islands with a stop at Snow Farm on your itinerary. If you do, you probably won't be the only one there dressed in Lycra—the vineyard is a popular stop for bicyclists.

Allenholm Orchards

Long before the vineyard opened, South Hero had a reputation for being an excellent place to grow apples. At one point it was home to

Crescent Bay Farm B&B

The Crescent Bay Farm Bed & Breakfast in South Hero has strong credentials as a place for weary travelers to find rest. After all, it was once the home of Horatio Jackson. Don't remember him? He was the Burlington doctor who in 1903 became the first person to drive across the United States. He made the journey east in a Winton Touring Car, which could crank out only 20 horsepower. Surviving blown tires, broken axles, and dust storms, Jackson made the trip in 63 days. When he returned to Burlington, he was pulled over by a police officer for speeding.

During the years Jackson lived at the house, he entertained well. His guests included Teddy Roosevelt, who enjoyed duck hunting on Lake Champlain. Also during this period, a farmhand named Harry Barber took to building miniature stone castles in the garden and at homes all over South Hero. They are still there today.

The property's history does not end with Jackson. Nor does it start there. The home was originally built in 1820 as a farmhouse. After Jackson's day, it belonged to the Norman family, who ran it as an inn during the 1950s, serving three meals a day to guests staying in roughly a dozen camps spread along the shore.

Today, the home, and the 112 acres that go with it, are again a farm. Dave Lane grew up there after his parents bought the place in 1961. Now he and his wife, Julie, raise about 50 Black Angus beef cattle and 10 llamas on the property and run the Crescent Bay Farm Bed & Breakfast.

The bed-and-breakfast is located just down the road from the Snow Farm Vineyard in South Hero. Visitors are more than welcome to pull over and admire the animals.

more than 100 orchards. Much of that crop was transported on canal boats south to New York City.

Just ahead on our tour are a pair of orchards that welcome visitors. To reach them from the winery, continue on down West Shore

Road for 2 miles until you reach South Street. Turn left. Drive up South Street for about a mile. Allenholm Orchards' store will be on your right.

Ray and Pam Allen's Allenholm Orchards is a diverse business, part apple orchard, part bake and gift shop, part petting zoo and part bed-and-breakfast—anything to sustain the farm that has been in Ray's family since 1870. The first apple trees were planted that year by Ray's great-grandfather, making them reputedly the oldest commercial orchard in Vermont.

Get out of your car at the Allens' place and you might be greeted by the braying of a donkey or the neighing of a horse. Both are part of the petting zoo, which also features a shaggy Scottish Highland cow, a miniature horse, sheep, goats, and rabbits. Next to the petting zoo are a playground and picnic tables where you can sit and eat the soft-serve ice cream ("creemees" to Vermonters) sold inside the farm store. You can also buy Vermont cheeses, jams, jellies, honey, pies, vegetables, and of course, fruit.

Hackett's Orchard

Just ahead on the other side of the road is Hackett's Orchard, where the Hacketts grow 47 varieties of apples, as well as many types of vegetables. Ron and Celia Hackett bought this farm about four decades ago, but it was already a well-established orchard when they took it over, having been started in 1900.

During their years in operation, Hackett's has become a local institution. With two orchards so close together, South Street is something of an apple alley in South Hero. Each October, the orchards sponsor an apple festival over Columbus Day weekend, which features craft shows, flea markets, and live music.

There are plenty of other reasons to visit Hackett's during summer or fall. In season, Hackett's offers pick-your-own apples. When you visit, you are welcome to tour the 14-acre orchard and have a bite to eat in the picnic area. There is no reason to go hungry at Hackett's Orchard, especially once you've smelled their fresh-baked pies and cider donuts.

If you continue up South Street, you will meet up with Route 2. Turn right and follow it south to Interstate 89, to head back to wherever you started this tour through this region of contrasts.

Boyden Valley Winery
Cambridge
802-644-8151
www.boydenvalley.com
Open Memorial Day through December, Tuesday through Sunday, 10 a.m. to 5 p.m. The rest of the year, the winery is open Friday through Sunday, 10 a.m. to 5 p.m.

Milk House Market
Cambridge
802-644-6363
Open Memorial Day through December, Tuesday through Sunday 10 a.m. to 5 p.m. The hours vary during the rest of the year. Call ahead to check. During the holidays, they sell turkey, pheasant, and Christmas trees.

Vermont Maple Outlet
Jeffersonville
800-858-3121
www.vermontmapleoutlet.com
Open daily, year-round, from 9 a.m. to 5 p.m.

Chester Arthur Homestead
Fairfield
802-828-3051
Open Wednesday through Sunday from 11 a.m. to 5 p.m. between late May and mid-October.

Green Mountain Blue Cheese
Highgate Center
802-868-4193
www.vtcheese.com/vtcheese/greenmtn/vtblue.htm
You are welcome to visit anytime. Since it is a farm,

someone is usually around to greet you. If no one is available, you can still find samples and cheese to buy.

Carman Brook Maple & Dairy Farm
Swanton
802-868-2347
www.cbmaplefarm.com
Open from 8:30 a.m. to 4:30 p.m., Tuesday through Saturday from March through mid-November. There is a maple open house during the first weekend of spring, which includes maple-related games, demonstrations of how Native Americans traditionally made syrup, and sugar on snow, which means hot, thickened syrup drizzled over snow to make it chewy like taffy. Each fall, the farm hosts a sugarhouse tea on the second Saturday in November. Check the Web site or phone for details and to learn about special events.

West Swanton Orchards, Farm Market, and Cider Mill
Swanton
802-868-9100
Open daily from 10 a.m. to 5 p.m. May through December,

selling apples, cider, pies, doughnuts, and souvenirs. Also offers pick-your-own apples in season.

Lakeside Berry Farm
East Alburg
802-796-3691
Open daily from 10 a.m. to 4:30 p.m. August through mid-October. Call ahead if you would like to pick your own raspberries after hours.

Lakes End Cheeses
Alburg
800-310-3730
www.lakesendcheeses.com
Open daily between Memorial Day and Labor Day from 10 a.m. to 4 p.m.

Hero's Welcome
North Hero
802-372-4161
www.heroswelcome.com
Open daily from 6:30 a.m. to 6:30 p.m. The deli closes at 5:30 p.m.

Snow Farm Vineyard
South Hero
802-372-9463
www.snowfarm.com
Open daily from 10 a.m. to

5 p.m., May 1 through
December 31. Tours of the
vineyard and winery are given
daily at 11 a.m. and 2 p.m. from
May through October. Tastings
are free and available anytime
during business hours. Call
ahead to arrange group tours.
Off-season visits are welcome;
just call ahead to make
arrangements.

Allenholm Orchards
South Hero
802-372-5566
www.allenholm.com
   Open daily from 9 a.m. to 5
p.m., Memorial Day through
December 24. Apples,
blueberries, raspberries,
pumpkins, and vegetables are
available in season.

Hackett's Orchard
South Hero
802-372-5555
   Open May through
December. Summer hours are 8
a.m. to 8 p.m. Hours are shorter
the rest of the year; call ahead for
details.

Restaurants

North Hero House
North Hero
888-525-3644
www.northherohouse.com
   Serves dinner seven days a
week in its elegant dining room
from April through October. The
food is contemporary American,
with entrées ranging from $14 to
$28.

Shore Acres Inn
& Restaurant
North Hero
802-372-8722
www.shoreacres.com
   Open weekends starting
around Easter, then serves dinner
seven days a week from early
May through October. In
November, the restaurant serves
dinner weekends only through
Thanksgiving. The dining room
offers glorious views of Lake
Champlain and the Green
Mountains to the east. The
menu runs the gamut from
gourmet to that Yankee favorite,
pot roast. Entrée items cost
between $13 and $27.

Sand Bar Inn
South Hero
802-372-6911
www.sandbarinn.com

Serves dinner year-round. The restaurant menu features fine American cuisine with entrées ranging from $14 to $25. There is also a bistro menu with items ranging from $5 to $12.

Lodging

The Tyler Place Family Resort
Highgate Springs
802-868-4000
www.tylerplace.com

Open Memorial Day weekend through Labor Day. An all-inclusive family resort on Lake Champlain. Rates, which are per person per day, range from $82 to $291 for adults and $61 to $99 for children, depending on the time of year.

North Hero House
North Hero
888-525-3644

Open April 15 through October. This inn, which sits beside Lake Champlain, offers elegant accommodations ranging from $95 to $295. Includes breakfast.

Shore Acres Inn
& Restaurant
North Hero
802-372-8722
www.shoreacres.com

Open mid-May through October. This lakeside inn with large grounds features tennis courts, nine holes of golf, swimming, and other amenities. Rooms are between $90 and $190, depending on size and season. Includes breakfast.

Crescent Bay Farm
Bed & Breakfast
South Hero
802-372-4807
www.crescentbaybb.com

Open May through October. Located on a historic working farm that raises Black Angus beef cattle and llamas. The farm overlooks Lake Champlain. Rooms cost $105 per night.

For additional lodging options, check the extensive listing at www.vermontvacation.com or call 800-VERMONT.

Northeastern Vermont

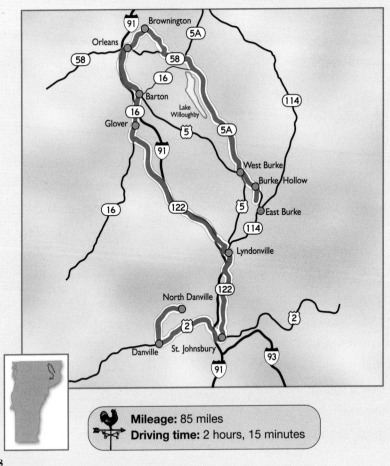

Mileage: 85 miles
Driving time: 2 hours, 15 minutes

The Northeast Kingdom

For more than half a century, Vermont has had a kingdom within its borders. The so-called Northeast Kingdom, located in the northeast corner of the state, is a kingdom in concept, not in fact. It is a place set apart from the rest of the state both physically and culturally.

George Aiken, Vermont's famed U.S. Senator and one-time governor, popularized the phrase in the late 1940s when he used it in an important speech. At the time, he was worried about out-of-state investors exploiting the area's many natural resources, especially its forests and rivers. Aiken was an avid fisherman who had a special fondness for the area, and he wanted to preserve the region's charms as a recreational area. Today, thanks to Aiken and other state and local leaders, when people speak of the Northeast Kingdom, Vermonters think of a place that has maintained the state's rural character and natural beauty.

Farming and forestry define this rugged region of hills, fields, and forests. The largest sections of farmland lie in a crescent-shaped swath that stretches roughly from Peacham to Hardwick to Craftsbury to Irasburg to Newport. In the center of that crescent are the great woodlands of Vermont, which are part of a forest that stretches through New Hampshire, all the way to Maine. The land-based economy has changed little here in the last several decades, giving the region a traditional Vermont look and feel.

When Aiken talked of the Northeast Kingdom, he was referring to Orleans, Caledonia, and Essex counties. Ever since that time, people have debated the boundaries of this mythical kingdom and have inevitably stretched them farther south and west as communities have begun to define themselves as part of the realm.

Whichever side you take in this boundary debate, you are definitely within the Kingdom when you reach Danville. That's where this tour will begin, before we head north through St. Johnsbury to Lyndonville, Glover, Barton, Brownington, and East Burke. Along the way, we will see an array of older farms that have recently adapted in order to entertain and accommodate visitors, as well as long-standing businesses that make consumer products from the farm and for the farm. We will also visit some of the historic sites that are reminders of the area's nineteenth-century grandeur.

(Our tour will take us through the south-central part of the Kingdom, visiting places that welcome visitors. If you want to take in more of this beautiful farming country, consider a drive along the edge of the agricultural crescent, starting in Peacham and then taking routes 16 and 14 through Hardwick, Craftsbury, Albany, Irasburg, Coventry and Newport. Tour 3 also visits a part of the Northeast Kingdom, East Hardwick and Greensboro.)

Danville is most easily reached by taking Route 2 East from

The Story of Maple Syrup

Maple sugaring season is something of a miracle. It couldn't happen if Vermont didn't have the perfect climate for it. It also couldn't happen if the trees didn't have a unique combination of traits: their sap runs for weeks, making it possible to create a large amount of syrup; they can easily survive the annual placement of a new tap into their bark; and, most important, their sap makes excellent syrup.

For as many years as Vermonters have been making maple syrup, much about the nature of sap production remains mysterious. We know that good sugaring weather requires cold nights and warm days, but some believe the wind also plays a factor. To remember the rule of thumb, they made up this easily remembered, though slightly tortured, rhyme:

> When the wind is in the west, the sap runs best.
> And when the wind is in the north, the sap runs forth.
> When the wind is in the south, the sap run drouth.
> And when the wind is in the east, the sap runs least.

Montpelier (it's about a 25-mile drive) or taking Route 2 West from St. Johnsbury (about an 8-mile drive).

↝ Danville

The town of Danville sits about as high in terms of altitude as any community in Vermont. You'll know that much from driving Route 2 East to the town. When you get to the center of the village, take a look around. What you'll see are clues to the prosperity that agriculture brought to this state in the nineteenth century. To your left is the imposing, columned town hall, showing just how seriously folks took their local government. To your right, is a large, lush green, which speaks to the community's belief in shared space.

In its earliest days, this small town turned out some of the most famous Vermonters, most notably Thaddeus Stevens, who pushed for abolition during the Civil War era and later led the drive to impeach President Andrew Johnson.

The Great Vermont Corn Maze

If you arrive in town anytime between August and late October and you need to stretch your legs, consider taking a detour to North Danville and the Great Vermont Corn Maze. To reach the maze, if you're heading east on Route 2, turn left at the blinking yellow light across from the green in the center of Danville. You'll be on Hill Street, which becomes the Bruce Badger Memorial Highway. In 5 miles you will reach North Danville. Turn left onto McReynolds Road and then right onto Old North Church Road, which you will follow for 3 miles until it dead-ends at Wheelock Road. Turn right. The Great Vermont Corn Maze is 1 mile down on the right at the Patterson Farm.

In addition to a seven-acre maze carved out of a cornfield, Dayna Boudreau and her husband, Michael, have created a series of farm-based games and activities on her family's dairy farm, including a smaller maze for young children, a petting zoo featuring miniature sheep and goats, and 100 feet of underground "gopher holes" for children to crawl through. There is also a barnyard golf course. Instead of golf clubs, players use cow clubs (ordinarily used for driving cows) to drive large plastic balls by such hazards as a laundry line or through a course of real horseshoes set up like croquet hoops.

If you're going to negotiate the maze, plan on about an hour and a half, which is the average time it takes people to make it through. If you run out of time or energy, don't worry: the maze includes "emergency exits."

Emergo Farm Bed & Breakfast

If you are looking for a place to stay while in the Danville area and want a real farm experience, try the Emergo Farm Bed & Breakfast.

The farm has been in the family of Bebo and Lori Webster for six generations, dating back to 1858. While there, you are welcome to take a tour of the 1897 barn and the modern milking parlor, or just kick back and relax on the porch.

To reach the farm, if you're driving east on Route 2 into the center of Danville, turn left onto Hill Street at the blinking light. In .6 mile, bear right onto Webster Hill Road. Emergo Farm B&B is the second house on the left.

To continue your tour after the corn maze, return to the center of Danville and head east again on Route 2. For the next 8 miles the road will rise and fall along a path that traverses the rolling countryside. Route 2 will then take you up one last small rise and into St. Johnsbury. The road will curve left and become the town's Main Street.

↭ St. Johnsbury

For years, St. Johnsbury was the industrial stronghold in an otherwise agricultural- and forestry-based region of the state. At the center of that industry was E. & T. Fairbanks and Company, the most commercially successful platform scale makers of the nineteenth century. The industry brought great wealth to the Fairbanks family, who shared it with their community.

St. Johnsbury Athenaeum

To see an example of the Fairbankses' sense of reciprocity, visit the St. Johnsbury Athenaeum, a combination public library and art gallery founded by the family. You'll see the Athenaeum on your left, shortly after you enter the downtown area—it's the imposing brick Victorian building just before the fire station. Park on Main Street near where Route 2 turns right and heads down Eastern Avenue.

Vermont Spirits

Vermont means different things to different people. To Duncan Holaday, it means milk, maple syrup, and vodka.

The entrepreneur arrived in Vermont in 1988, having spent his professional life as an academic. But Holaday wanted to follow a more earthly pursuit in Vermont. He wanted to find a way to live off the land.

So after building a solar home on an old farmstead near St. Johnsbury, Holaday found an unconventional use for the milk and maple the state is famous for. He would make vodkas with elements of each. Milk and maple might seem like strange components to use in making vodka. The spirit is commonly made with potatoes, wheat, or rye, but it doesn't have to be that way. To make vodka, all you need is something with sugar that the yeast can convert to alcohol.

For Holaday, the going wasn't always easy. The first distillery went up in flames after a cat knocked over the still. But the second distillery currently generates three types of vodka under his Vermont Spirits label: Gold Vodka, made with maple sap and distilled water; White Vodka, made with pure milk sugar and Vermont spring water; and Blue Vodka, made with pure cane sugar and Vermont spring water.

So vodka is the latest product to come from Vermont's hills and valleys. What will they think of next?

(To learn more about Vermont Spirits, check them out online at www.vermontspirits.com.)

The gallery includes paintings by members of the Hudson River School and the massive and spectacular "Domes of the Yosemite" by Albert Bierstadt, which takes up an entire wall.

Fairbanks Museum & Planetarium

Another block and a half down on Main Street, on the right, is the Fairbanks Museum and Planetarium, founded by the family in

1889. Although the museum has started to modernize, the place maintains much of the quirky character with which its Victorian-era founders imbued it.

The main gallery is loaded with a stunning array of taxidermy posed artfully in fabulous dioramas crafted more than a century ago. Upstairs, cases are filled with exotica donated by the Fairbankses and their friends—everything from carved ivory figures from Japan to portraits fashioned entirely from insects to a checkerboard looted from the home of Confederate President Jefferson Davis. Downstairs is the Eye on the Sky weather station, home of the state's best-known meteorologists. It features educational displays on climate.

The Fairbankses' prosperity and generosity gave the town a grandeur unheard of in most other communities of this size. Today, St. Johnsbury has a population of roughly 7,600, a small community in most states, but in the Northeast Kingdom it is the largest.

Return to Route 2 (Eastern Avenue) and follow it down the hill to Railroad Street (Route 2/5) and turn left. Follow Route 2 through the downtown and as it turns right, across a bridge. In 1 mile you will reach the Maple Grove Farms of Vermont factory, a large brick building on your right.

Maple Grove Farms of Vermont

Maple Grove is one of the state's largest producers of maple syrup, maple candies, salad dressings, marinades, sauces, you name it. But they manage to make the operation feel small and personal. Perhaps that's because nearly everyone in the community seems to have worked there at some time in their lives, and some have been there most of their lives. The place is something of a time capsule. Using technologies invented in the 1930s, workers mold maple candies, letting them dry overnight before inspecting and hand packing them into boxes. The adjacent gift shop sells everything made in the factory. An old sugarhouse, which sits on the lawn between the gift shop and the factory, offers a primer on how maple syrup is produced each spring. Appropriately, the displays explain both modern techniques and old-fashioned ones.

When you've finished touring Maple Grove Farms, get back on Route 2 heading west and proceed for 1 mile across the bridge and back into downtown St. Johnsbury. At the stop sign, turn right onto Route 5 North, on which you will follow the Passumpsic River out of town. Any farms that might formerly have hugged the edges of the river have long since been replaced by the sprawl that is starting to connect St. Johnsbury to Lyndonville.

↜ Lyndonville

Following Route 5 North for 9 miles, you will reach Lyndonville, a town that came into being in 1866 after a fire in St. Johnsbury gutted the workshops of the Connecticut and Passumpsic Rivers Railroad. Lyndonville grew up, and prospered, because of the relocated train terminus.

Miss Lyndonville Diner

Just before you enter downtown Lyndonville on Route 5, on the right you'll pass the Miss Lyndonville Diner. Actually, don't. If you are at all hungry, you'll want to stop. The restaurant is a local institution and has an almost cult following among visitors to the region. It is famed for its good diner fare, served fast and in large portions, but the diner is perhaps best known for its pies, especially its strawberry-blueberry pie, served only in berry season. There is an old story that years ago several academics were debating the meaning of the word "Yankee." Unable to agree on a definition, they called a world expert on such matters, poet Robert Frost, who offered a pithy reply: "A Yankee is someone who eats pie for breakfast." So if you happen by the diner in time for breakfast, stop in and try the pie, and become a Yankee, for a moment at least.

Bag Balm

As you enter Lyndonville, you'll see a building on the right that seems to have a giant tin of Bag Balm protruding from it. Fittingly, it is the offices of the Dairy Association Co., makers of Bag Balm. If you don't know about the stuff, Bag Balm is an all-purpose skin treatment for cuts, scrapes, or just dry skin. It is as versatile as duct tape. Bag Balm was invented by a Vermonter in 1899 and was intended only for use with animals. But the animals' owners inevitably tried it on their own skin and found the stuff too good not to borrow.

The factory, which offers tours, is just a few blocks away from the office building. Follow Route 5 to the stop sign at Depot Street, where the road turns to the left. You, however, should turn right, cross the railroad tracks, and take an immediate left. The factory is the grey building on the right. You can't miss it; it too has a giant tin of Bag Balm sticking out of it.

✦ Glover

From Lyndonville we will head over to the town of Glover, which is best known as the home of an innovative political puppet theater, but which also features several interesting businesses.

To reach Glover, follow Route 5 North out of Lyndonville. You will come quickly to a junction with Route 122. Turn left onto Route 122 and follow it northwest for 14 miles to the junction with Route 16. Route 122 runs roughly parallel to Interstate 91, but offers a slower pace and nicer scenery as it makes its way through a small farming valley. The road follows a narrow, heavily wooded valley and passes through the small towns of Wheelock and Sheffield. Wheelock and Sheffield are small communities, with a total of about 1,300 residents between them. Wheelock, by the way, was granted to Dartmouth College President John Wheelock and the school's trustees. Under the management, which lasted until the mid-1800s, rents paid by Wheelock residents helped support the college, which is located nearby in New Hampshire. In the 1930s, the state of Vermont and Dartmouth struck a deal whereby any Wheelock resident accepted to the school could attend for free.

Bread and Puppet

About half a mile before the junction of Routes 122 and 16, you will pass the Bread and Puppet Theater Museum. Started largely in protest of the Vietnam War, the iconoclastic and decidedly political puppet troupe held its annual Domestic Resurrection Circus from 1974 to 1998 in the large fields nearby. The circus drew crowds of thousands. Today, the troupe has decided to perform smaller pieces before smaller crowds at the site, and continues to travel nationally for protests/performances. The museum artfully displays the larger-than-life puppets that are the group's hallmark.

Currier's Quality Market

At the junction of Routes 122 and 16, turn right and follow Route 16 North for 1.5 miles into the center of the tiny town of Glover. If you are in need of food, drink, or pretty much anything, stop at Currier's Quality Market, on your left. It is a convenience store/grocery store/butcher shop/hardware store/place to catch up on local gossip. It is also certainly one of the few stores in America willing to give up retail space to make room for a stuffed moose, bear, timber wolf, bobcat, and several deer. All-in-one stores like Currier's serve an important function in remote areas like Glover, where shopping opportunities don't exactly abound.

Labour of Love

As you head north out of town on Route 16, there are a couple more stops you might want to make. One mile out of town you'll see Labour of Love, a nursery and garden. Kate Kennedy Butler has restored a nineteenth-century Greek Revival home and opened it to the public. On her grounds, Butler grows about 600 varieties of perennials. Extensive display gardens show you what your plants will look like in a formal setting. Labour of Love offers picnic tables where you can sit and get a good view of the Barton River, which runs beside the property.

Sugarwoods Farm

From Labour of Love, continue north on Route 16. If you are running low on maple treats, stop .3 miles down the road at Sugarwoods Farm on the right. Though they don't offer tours of their production facility, the folks at Sugarwoods do have a small gift shop where they sell all their products.

◦ Brownington

Next, we'll visit a remarkable building made by a remarkable man in the midst of what was then a recently settled farming community. Heading north out of Glover on Route 16, go another 2 miles from Sugarwoods Farms until you reach Barton. There, pick up Route 5 North and follow it for about 3 miles into Orleans. Route 5 will "T" with Route 58. Turn right onto Route 58 East, and drive through the downtown area. About a quarter mile after leaving the commercial district, bear left onto East Street. You will follow this road into Brownington. The name of the road will change as you cross town lines, so don't be concerned that you are lost when you see street signs marked Tarbox Hill Road or Frog Pond Road. It is all the same road.

Old Stone House Museum

Upon entering the village of Brownington, turn right onto the dirt
road (Old Stone House Road) when you reach the church. You will
see the Old Stone House Museum just ahead on your right.

The imposing four-story granite building may seem wildly out of
place in the middle of a field in a sleepy rural Vermont town, but
Brownington was decidedly less sleepy when the building was constructed in the 1830s. At the time, the town was a half-shire town,
taking turns with the town of Craftsbury as seat of the county court.

The building served as a dormitory for the Orleans County
Grammar School. Perhaps housing the students in such a grand
building was meant to suggest to them that what they did mattered.

The Old Stone House was designed by Alexander Twilight, pur-
ported to have been the nation's first African-American college grad-
uate and state legislator. He was nothing if not an impressive builder.
The massive structure, requiring 750,000 tons of granite, was constructed in the 1830s. It was the state's first granite building, pre-
dating the State House by a couple of years.

Legend has it that Twilight built the massive structure with only
the help of an ox and a pry bar. Anecdotal evidence and common
sense, however, suggest he must have had help. The organization that
preserves the building uses it to display local history.

Across the street, the museum recently added the Lawrence
Barn, which was moved to the site from the nearby town of Albany,
where it had stood for more than a century and a half. Fittingly, the
barn houses a display on the evolution of farming in Orleans County
during the last two centuries.

Prospect Hill

If you want to get a better sense of where you are, turn right when
you return to the pavement after leaving the Old Stone House Museum. Now take an immediate left at the entrance to Prospect Hill.
The hill is named for the broad view it offers. Park your car here and

walk to the top, or drive there if you prefer. At the top, you will find a small wooden tower from which you will have a 360-degree view that takes in Lake Willoughby to the south and Canada to the north.

Once we leave Prospect Hill, we will head back along the paved road the way we came. Follow the main road. This time, however, do not turn back onto Frog Pond Road when you see the sign on your right in half a mile. Instead, continue straight for a little more than 2 miles. When you meet Route 58, turn left and follow that road south for about 5 miles to the junction with Route 5A. Turn right and follow Route 5A South for about 12 miles as it passes

Lake Willoughby

For sublime beauty, it's hard to beat Lake Willoughby. Squeezed between two towering mountains, the lake resembles nothing so much as a Scottish loch. The peaks, Mount Pisgah and Mount Hor, take their names from the Old Testament and have a raw splendor to them. Standing like bookends at the south end of the lake, they tower more than 1,500 feet above it. The mountains' sheer cliffs might seem inhospitable, but they are home to peregrine falcons.

The entire setting is the work of a glacier, which cut the five-mile-long lake from an existing valley some 12,000 years ago. Much of the glacier's work is invisible. The lake's waters reach a depth of more than 300 feet, making it one of the deepest in New England.

For all its beauty, Lake Willoughby is relatively lightly developed. Lakeside cottages and motels are located along the northeastern shore. Route 5A runs across the flank of the hills along the eastern shore. The steep terrain around much of the rest of the lake makes development there virtually impossible. The easiest spots to reach the water are at the north or south ends, where there are beaches.

through a mix of wooded and open land, punctuated by the occasional farm. The road will snake along the east side of stunning Lake Willoughby, whose southern end squeezes between the towering cliffs of Mount Pisgah and Mount Hor. Continue south on Route 5A to its junction with Route 5 in West Burke. From there we'll travel back roads to East Burke.

↝ East Burke

We are headed south, toward a former farm in East Burke that once supplied ingredients to one of New York City's finest hotels. Today the farm has been reincarnated as an inn. To reach the Inn at Mountain View Farm, follow the paved Burke Hollow Road (near where Routes 5 and 5A meet) for about 2 miles through Burke Hollow and to the top of the hill, where you'll turn right onto Darling Hill Road. Follow this ridgetop road for another 2 miles, and just past the "T" intersection with East Darling Hill Road, turn right into the parking lot.

The Inn at Mountain View Farm
The 440-acre Mountain View Farm was built in 1883 by Elmer Darling and once supplied meat and dairy products to his stylish Fifth Avenue Hotel in New York City. Today the farm has been converted into a 14-bedroom inn and a restaurant that is open to the public. Before dinner most Friday and Saturday nights, or by special arrangement, the inn offers horse-drawn wagon or sleigh rides through the farm's pastures and over its hills.

Viewing the surrounding mountains after eating dinner or while taking a wagon ride at the inn, you might feel like you are the lord or lady of the Kingdom.

You can return to Danville via Route 5, I-89, and Route 2 West.

The Great Corn Maze

North Danville
802-748-1399
www.vermontcornmaze.com

The Great Corn Maze season runs roughly from August 1 to the second to last Sunday in October. The petting zoo, tunnels, and smaller maze open on the second Saturday in July (if the corn is high enough). Open from 10 a.m. to 5 p.m., from the opening of the season through September. Visitors are not allowed to enter the maze after 4 p.m. In October, the business closes at 4 p.m., and visitors are not allowed into the maze after 3 p.m. Call in case of inclement weather. Admission, which includes the mazes, petting zoo, and tunnels, is $8 for people 15 and older; $6 for children ages 4 to 14. Children under 4 get in free. A round of barnyard golf costs $3 per person. Check the Web site for special events.

St. Johnsbury Athenaeum

St. Johnsbury
802-748-8291
www.stjathenaeum.org

Open Monday and Wednesday 10 a.m. to 8 p.m.; Tuesday, Thursday, and Friday 10 a.m. to 5:30 p.m.; and Saturday 9:30 a.m. to 4 p.m.

Fairbanks Museum & Planetarium

St. Johnsbury
802-748-2372
www.fairbanksmuseum.org

Open Monday through Saturday 9 a.m. to 5 p.m.; Sunday 1 to 5 p.m. Admission: Adults $5; senior citizens $4; children ages 5 to 17, $3; children under 5, free. Families (immediate family only) maximum of 3 adults, no limit on number of children, $12.

Maple Grove Farms of Vermont

St. Johnsbury
802-748-5141
www.maplegrove.com

Factory tours are offered Monday through Friday from 8 a.m. to 2 p.m. Get there as early as possible if you want to see the workers at their busiest.

Bag Balm Factory
Lyndonville
802-626-5327
   Tours are available while the factory is running, weekdays from 8 a.m. to noon and 12:30 to 2:30 p.m. If you are making a special trip, call ahead to make sure the factory is in operation that day.

Bread and Puppet
Glover
802-525-3031
   The museum is open each summer through October. The group does not have its own Web site. Call to check on upcoming events, museum hours, or to arrange an off-season visit to the museum.

Currier's Quality Market
Glover
802-525-8822

Labour of Love
Glover
802-525-6695

Sugarwoods Farm
Glover
802-525-3718
800-245-3718
   The gift shop is open Monday through Friday 8 a.m. to 5 p.m.

Old Stone House Museum
Brownington
802-754-2022
www.oldstonehousemuseum.org
   Open Wednesday through Saturday from 11 a.m. to 5 p.m., from May 15 to October 15. Admission: adults, $5; children under 12, $4.

Restaurants

Miss Lyndonville Diner
Lyndonville
802-626-9890
   Open Monday through Thursday 6 a.m. to 8 p.m.; Friday and Saturday 6 a.m. to 9 p.m.; and Sunday 7 a.m. to 8 p.m. Serving classic diner food, plus homemade dinners like meat loaf, roast turkey, and prime rib. Most entrées range from $5 to $8. The entire menu is available all day.

Inn at Mountain View Farm
East Burke
802-626-9924
800-572-4509
www.innmtnview.com
   Dinner served Wednesday through Sunday in the winter and every night except Tuesday

in the summer. Entrées cost between $15 to $26. Reservations are recommended.

Elements Food and Spirit

St. Johnsbury
802-748-8400
www.elementsfood.com

This restaurant serves modern American food in a converted mill overlooking the Passumpsic River. Dinner served year-round Tuesday through Thursday 5 to 9 p.m., Friday and Saturday 5 to 9:30 p.m.; Entrées range from $13 to $22. Lunch served Memorial Day through Columbus Day, Tuesday through Friday 11:30 a.m. to 1:30 p.m.

Lodging

Emergo Farm Bed & Breakfast

Danville
888-383-1185
www.emergofarm.com

The room rate for a couple is $90 a night. For the family suite, rates start at $115 and are based on the number of people.

WilloughVale Inn

Westmore
802-525-4123
800-594-9102
www.willoughvaleinn.com

The inn, which sits beside picturesque Lake Willoughby, is open year-round and offers rooms and cottages ranging from $85 to $250 per night, depending on size and season.

Inn at Mountain View Farm

East Burke
802-626-9924
800-572-4509
www.innmtnview.com

Room rates range from $155 to $255. Breakfast is prepared for guests, who can also request a packed gourmet lunch.

For additional lodging options, check the extensive listings at www.vermontvacation.com or call 800-VERMONT.

Central Vermont
Northern Sector

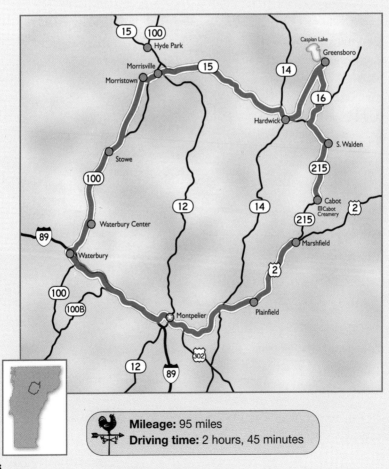

Mileage: 95 miles
Driving time: 2 hours, 45 minutes

Old Traditions
and New Pathways

asual visitors to central Vermont can be forgiven
if they view the northern-central part of the state
as something other than agricultural. After all, the
twin cities of Barre and Montpelier tend to overshadow the
surrounding towns and neither would be confused with a
farming community. Both cities have their own claims to
fame—Montpelier as the seat of state government, Barre as
the heart and soul of the American granite industry—but
there is much more to central Vermont.

You don't have to travel far outside either city before you
begin to see farms where most cities would have densely
packed suburbs. In truth, the farms used to begin closer to

the city centers. But lagging milk prices and rising real estate values have conspired to push farmers off the land.

Economic pressures have not driven farmers from central Vermont, but farmers there have been forced to adapt in order to survive. Many have diversified their operations to create new revenue streams and to bring some much needed stability to their farms. Sometimes it means running new agricultural businesses alongside the old dairy operation, or evolving to meet the increasing demand for products such as organic goods. Other times it means strengthening existing bonds between farmers to make milk-based foods such as cheese and yogurt.

This tour will show you the range of choices farmers have made to keep their land working. It will also introduce you to other Vermonters who are keeping small parcels of land open through their horticultural businesses.

We will start in the rich agricultural country around Cabot, where farms lie along the flanks of low hills. First we will visit Vermont's best-known cheese company. From there, we will stop at several perennial gardens that have developed a loyal following. The terrain will become wooded and the valleys narrow before things open up and become distinctly mountainous as we head south through the broad alpine valley containing Stowe. South of Stowe we will stop at the Ben & Jerry's ice cream factory and a popular nearby cider mill. We will then drive east through a slender river valley to reach the state capitol, finishing the tour by stopping at three long-standing farms that have adapted their businesses to welcome visitors.

Blunt Advice

In the early 1900s, a periodical named *The Hill Country of Northern New England* had this rather blunt advice for farmers:

"Some there are in New England who declare that it is not cows we should milk, but city people. The latter come with full money bags, overflowing. . . . What more should we ask unless it were manna from Heaven?"

If you want to visit most of the stops suggested on the tour, you may want to budget two days. Otherwise, you might feel rushed.

↷ Cabot

A logical place to begin is in the farming town of Cabot. At the core of the community is the renowned creamery that takes its name from the town. To get there, take Route 2 to Marshfield then turn onto Route 215 North. (If you are coming from Montpelier or Barre, it is a left-hand turn. From St. Johnsbury, it is a right.) As you head north, you will pass numerous farms (they are Cabot owner-members). Four miles out of Marshfield on Route 215 you will reach the creamery, which will be on your right.

Cabot Creamery

The Cabot Creamery is living proof of the value of cooperation. The full name of the organization is the Cabot Creamery Cooperative, because the farm families that ship their milk there are actually owner-members of the co-op. This is not some new idea; local farmers founded the co-op more than eighty-five years ago. Just as they are today, farmers then were struggling due to low milk prices. So they banded together to increase their clout in the market and to demand higher prices.

The idea is the same today, but along the way Cabot members have added a new strategy to that original idea: they decided to begin making and selling their own cheese and then sharing the profits among themselves. That's nothing new either. The cooperative began producing cheese in 1930. Today's cheese operation, however, is nothing like it used to be. Cabot is now the largest producer of cheddar in the state and sells its many types of cheddar and other cheeses nationwide, concentrating most heavily on the East Coast.

Enter the Creamery via the gift shop. There you will find all

Cheddar Cheese

If it seems that Vermonters have been making cheddar cheese since, well, before they were Vermonters, you're right. Cheddar cheese is in fact a bit older than Vermont, about 600 years older.

That might help to explain why the cheese is almost synonymous with the state. When British colonists began moving into Vermont starting in the mid-1700s, they brought with them what they knew. And one of those things was how to make cheddar. As cheese recipes go, it is a simple recipe,and it originated in the English town of Cheddar. (Ironically, no one in Cheddar makes cheddar anymore.)

But Vermonters didn't make cheddar just because it was rather straightforward to make. They also took to the cheese because it was durable, in more ways than one. First off, the cheese is hard, so it is easily transported. Somehow Brie doesn't seem suited for the rough-and-tumble life on the frontier. Cheddar also ages well, so you could make the cheese when you had the time and the milk on hand and eat it months later. At a time when food could be scarce in the winter, an enduring cheese was hard to overvalue.

Today, because of that tradition, Vermont remains a stronghold for cheddar making. The Cabot Creamery Cooperative is perhaps the state's best-known producer and regularly receives national and international awards for its cheddar, but Cabot also champions the cause of all Vermont cheesemakers through its involvement in the Vermont Cheese Council. The Grafton Village Cheese Company and Shelburne Farms are also members who make celebrated cheddars. Currently there are over 30 member cheesemakers in Vermont, many of whom create their own fine versions of the classic cheese.

Perhaps there is one last reason that Vermonters are so keen on making cheddar: It goes so well with that other old Yankee tradition, apple pie.

manner of Vermont-made food products, from coffees to jams to mustards, and, of course, cheese. The folks at Cabot are happy to let you try before you buy. They offer samples of their roughly two dozen types of award-winning cheddar—from classic varieties, ranging from mild to extra sharp, to newer creations flavored with chipotle peppers, smoky bacon, roasted garlic, you name it—as well as the other cheeses they make. Incidentally, Cabot also produces whipped cream, yogurt, butter, and dips.

Make time to take the tour of the factory. Exploring the plant, you may be struck by how intimate an essentially industrial space can feel. As you enter the production area, you'll notice photos of member-owners proudly displayed on the walls. Ask around and you'll soon learn that many employees here have spent most of their working lives at the co-op. Something about the place breeds loyalty. Viewing the production areas will answer the question of how Cabot manages to make so much cheese and do it so well. Computer-controlled machines have taken over the most physically demanding jobs, leaving employees to tackle the tasks that affect quality most.

It is hard to overestimate the impact Cabot has on the Vermont landscape. In 1992 Cabot merged with Agri-Mark, another New England dairy cooperative, and today they count 450 Vermont farm families as members, or approximately one-quarter of all dairy farms in the Green Mountain State. So when consumers across the country buy Cabot products, they are helping maintain the agricultural character of Vermont.

⌁ East Hardwick and Greensboro

While Cabot's success has enabled countless farmers to keep their fields open, some central Vermonters have found other ways to contribute to the working landscape. Among those are many gardeners who have turned a passion into a business, selling perennials suitable for Vermont and other, more forgiving climates. Our tour now takes us through a lightly farmed and wooded area to East Hardwick and Greensboro to visit two of these perennial purveyors. The Hardwick area is the commercial center for the area's farming population, and at the turn of the twentieth century the town was known as the "Granite Center of the World." The quarries were abandoned during the Depression. In contrast, Greensboro is a rural village on Caspian Lake, and a favorite summer retreat for vacationers.

Perennial Pleasures Nursery

Our first stop will be the aptly named Perennial Pleasures in East Hardwick, a combination plant store, teahouse, and gift shop that features gardening books, women's clothing, jewelry, and tea sets.

To get there from Cabot Creamery, continue north on Route 215 straight through the center of Cabot. Half a mile out of town bear left where the road forks, following the sign to South Walden Road. After 5.4 miles, turn left onto Route 15 West and follow that road for 2.4 miles until you reach Route 16 North, where you will turn right. After 1.5 miles turn left onto Main Street at the sign for East Hardwick. Go straight through the village, cross the bridge, and bear left. Perennial Pleasures Nursery and Tea Garden is immediately on your left.

The first thing you might notice, if you frequent large garden centers, is how welcome you feel at Perennial Pleasures and other locally owned plant stores in Vermont. Open May through September, Perennial Pleasures specializes in heirloom flowering plants and herbs. Owners Judith and Rachel Kane, who are mother and daughter, respectively, have planted three acres of demonstration gardens for customers to wander. If you need time to ponder a purchase, or just want refreshment, try the afternoon English cream tea, served from noon to 4 p.m. indoors, or, weather permitting, in the garden. Reservations are suggested.

Vermont Daylilies

The next stop is Vermont Daylilies in Greensboro. To get there, exit Perennial Pleasures' parking area, turn right, and then take an immediate left, just before the bridge, onto East Church Street. Follow this road for 3.3 miles until you reach a stop sign. Turn right onto Breezy Avenue. Half a mile down on your right you will see Vermont Daylilies.

As the name suggests, the place specializes in daylilies. In fact, there are more than 700 varieties, along with hundreds of other kinds of perennials. Local horticulturists Lewis and Nancy Hill launched the business more than thirty years ago. It is now owned by Kathy Unser and her husband, John Hunt, who continue to sell unique hybrids created by Lewis Hill. These varieties include hybrids Hill named in honor of local residents, who included Nan Rehnquist (wife of the U.S. Supreme Court's chief justice, who is a summer resident in Greensboro) and members of a 4-H club Hill directed.

Vermont Daylilies is open from Memorial Day through Labor Day, although you can find Kathy and John at the garden most days in May, when they are busy potting. The garden tends to peak between the middle of July and the first week of August.

Willey's Store

If you need a snack (or pretty much anything else), head down to Willey's Store on Main Street, a Greensboro institution catering to residents and summer visitors. The general store stocks everything from hammers to bait to steak to wine.

While you are in town, if the weather is hot, consider taking a dip in Caspian Lake. The public beach and changing rooms are across the street from Willey's Store.

↭ Hyde Park and Morrisville

From Greensboro we head to Hyde Park, where our next stop will be Applecheek Farm, which arranges backwoods treks for visitors. You'll need to call ahead for reservations, but it is worth it.

To reach Hyde Park, drive back down Breezy Avenue away from

the center of Greensboro. In less than a mile, the road will become Center Road and later Maple Street. Continue straight for about 6 miles until you reach the town of Hardwick. Turn left onto North Main Street. Just ahead at the light you will reach the junction of Routes 14 and 15. Turn right onto Route 15 West. The road will snake along, crisscrossing the Lamoille River, whose path it roughly follows. About 5 miles out of Hardwick, on your left you will see the Fisher Covered Railroad Bridge, which was built in 1908. The cupola on top was designed to allow the smoke from steam trains to escape. Trapped smoke is no longer a concern as the rail line has been abandoned. Biking and walking enthusiasts hope to convert the rail line for recreational use.

How the land is used in this stretch of the Lamoille Valley is not obvious. Most of the land-based work done in this area is undertaken far from the road, where loggers cut trees for the paper and wood-products industries.

Applecheek Farm

As you drive west along Route 15, the tight, wooded valley will begin to open up and make room for farms, like Applecheek Farm. To get there, from the Fisher Covered Railroad Bridge drive 7.5 miles then turn right onto Garfield Road, which rises gradually from the valley. Follow the road 1.8 miles until you reach McFarlane Road. Turn right and follow the road to the end, where you'll find the 327-acre Applecheek Farm, which sits above the valley and offers glorious views of Mount Mansfield, Camel's Hump, and the mountains of the Worcester Range of the Green Mountains.

John and Judy Clark have owned the farm for about 40 years. Like many dairy farmers before them, they found that milking cows simply didn't pay the bills. So they found a novel way to diversify. In addition to taking their dairy farm organic, they began to offer all means of animal-powered rides through the woods and fields that make up the farm. Today visitors can take a llama-drawn cart ride or a horse-drawn wagon ride. The more adventurous can sign up for a llama trek or a winter sleigh ride. The Clarks also sell maple syrup from their trees, processed and unprocessed fiber from their llamas, and meat, oil, leather, and eggs from the emus they raise.

You can also ask for a farm tour and, if you have a large group or bus tour, you can rent the upstairs of the barn, which the Clarks have converted into a meeting hall. Because theirs is a working farm, they ask that you call ahead before visiting. If your group wants to have a meal at the farm, the Clarks can arrange for that, too: their son runs a catering business.

Next we will visit a high-quality local nursery in Morrisville that attracts people from all over. To get to Morrisville, return to Route 15 via Garfield Road. Turn right and continue west on Route 15.

Cady's Falls Nursery

To reach the nursery from Applecheek Farm, stay on Route 15 for 2 miles. After going straight at the traffic light in Morrisville, you will take a slight left onto Needle Eye Road. Follow this road for 2.8 miles, at which point it will fork. Bear left and then turn left over the bridge. After crossing the bridge, take an immediate right onto Duhamel Road. In 1.6 miles, you will see a driveway cut through a row of trees. This is the entrance to the nursery.

Lela and Don Avery opened Cady's Falls Nursery more than 20 years ago. They specialize in hardy perennials for cold climates like Vermont's. If customers want to get some ideas for a formal garden, they can walk through the nursery to the beautiful, elegant gardens that sit behind a restored old farmhouse and barn. The barn provides a workspace for the nursery, a sort of potting shed extraordinaire.

The nursery is one of those hidden gems you can find on the back roads of Vermont. Others are more obvious, but also worth a visit. The next two stops—the Cold Hollow Cider Mill and the Ben & Jerry's ice cream factory in Waterbury Center—are among the most popular destinations in the state.

↝ Waterbury Center via Stowe

To reach Waterbury Center from Cady's Falls Nursery, drive back down Duhamel Road. When you reach the bridge, instead of crossing it, turn right. In a quarter mile, turn right onto Stagecoach Road, which rises to the top of a hill and offers grand views of the mountains of Stowe and beyond. In 7 miles you'll reach the junction with Route 100. Turn right and follow Route 100 South through the center of Stowe, which you'll reach in a mile and a half.

Although tourism has long dominated Stowe, the town manages to maintain its charm. As you leave Stowe and head toward Waterbury, you will notice tourist offerings jostling for space with farmland. Tourism is a valuable addition to the Vermont economy, but in areas like Stowe it can make farming more difficult by driving up the cost of land. As a result, tourist towns like Stowe find it difficult to hold on to working farms that help keep the land open.

Cold Hollow Cider Mill

Six miles south of Stowe village on Route 100 you will see the Cold Hollow Cider Mill on your left. The mill is New England's largest producer of fresh cider and draws roughly 300,000 customers each year. Inside, visitors can watch the cider being pressed from locally grown apples, and they can shop in the large adjacent store for such Vermont-made foods as jellies, cheeses, fudge, honey, and fresh-made cider donuts. The store always offers a variety of spreads and dips for customers to sample.

Ben & Jerry's Factory

Just down the road from the cider mill is Ben & Jerry's. To get there, turn left out of the cider mill parking lot and continue south on Route 100 for 2.5 miles. The factory will be on your right.

Company co-founder Jerry Greenfield once asked: "If it's not fun, why do it?" The factory has seemingly taken these words as its credo. The place is whimsically painted, much like the company's ice cream cartons. Walls are sky blue and accented with black and white cows and puffy white clouds. The lighthearted theme continues in the company store and scoop shop, as well as during the factory tour, which introduces visitors to new flavors and pays homage to dearly departed ones.

The humor can sometimes obscure the fact that Ben & Jerry's plays an important role in the state's agriculture. Since it was founded in 1978, the company has been one of the largest buyers of Vermont milk, helping create a demand for fluid milk that helps keep the price of milk up for farmers.

From here, we'll head to the state capital, Montpelier, where we'll visit the State House.

◇ Montpelier

To reach Montpelier you'll continue south on Route 100 through the village of Waterbury, where it will meet Route 2. Just outside the village, Route 100 will branch right. You want to continue going straight on Route 2, which will take you along the Winooski River and past some pretty farmland. In about 15 minutes, you'll find yourself in downtown Montpelier. What will strike you first is how small Montpelier is. Its population barely crests 8,000, but it has the feel of a larger community, with a strong downtown retail district full of stores selling both funky and essential items. The city is also home to the New England Culinary Institute (NECI), which operates three restaurants in Montpelier and several others in the Burlington area. There are numerous other eateries as well.

Vermont State House

When you reach the traffic light, you will be on State Street. Continue going straight as you pass through the nation's smallest state capital (by population). If you need to stretch your legs, park near

Farmers Diner

Walk into the Farmers Diner and you'll see the phrase on menus, t-shirts, and mugs: "food from here." That's the restaurant's motto, and its founder hopes it will help change the way America eats, while at the same time helping preserve family farms. Tod Murphy, who is himself a farmer, launched the restaurant in 2002 in the city of Barre in hopes of creating a food revolution. The message is everywhere.

Just look at the menus, which feature photographs of the local small-scale farmers who produce the food. There's Monty Adams, a rancher in nearby Starksboro, who raises beef for the restaurant. So the burger on your plate came from about 30 miles away, not 1,500 miles away like the average burger in this country.

Keeping the food supply close means that most of the diner's money is spent in the community. So far, the diner has found enough local suppliers that 65 cents out of every dollar it spends on food goes to a farmer or small-scale food producer within 70 miles of the restaurant.

Murphy hopes eventually to take this model nationwide. In his plan, the Barre diner is the first of three or four he'd like to see in Vermont, and from there he'd like to build at least 400 across the country.

If you want to get in on the act, you'll find the Farmers Diner on Main Street in Barre. Call them at 802-476-7623, or look them up at www.farmersdiner.com. Bon appétit.

the gold-domed capitol and take a tour. Guides are available, but you may tour the building yourself if you prefer. For years, the Legislature was made up largely of farmers. As the number of farms has diminished, so has the number of farmer-legislators. Now lawyers and other professionals far outnumber farmers in the State House.

If you'd like a snack, you may want to stop at any of Montpelier's many restaurants. But if you'd prefer to treat yourself to some beautiful countryside while you eat, you have a couple of choices.

Morse Farm Maple Sugarworks

The first is Morse Farm, which is easily reached from downtown Montpelier. From the State House, simply continue into the center of town on State Street and turn left onto Main Street at the stoplight. Bear right at the traffic rotary to continue on Main Street, and after 2.5 miles you will see Morse Farm on the right.

The farm has been in the same family for seven generations. Burr Morse, who runs the farm business now, has converted the operation into a major attraction for skiers and outdoor recreation enthusiasts. The farm still makes maple syrup each spring and sells all kinds of Vermont-made foods. Maple creemees and maple kettle popcorn are among the farm's specialties, and are both worth trying.

The Morses recently began putting their land to a new use — they hired a former Olympic cross-country ski racer to design trails through their woods. Now Morse Farm brings in extra income from skiing in the winter and mountain biking in the summer.

Bragg Farm

Next up is another farm that still makes maple syrup but has opened itself to visitors. To get there, return to Montpelier on Main Street, and when you come to the light keep going straight. (If you didn't visit Morse Farm, you would drive down State Street to the light at Main, and turn right.) Cross the bridge and turn left onto Route 2 East. As you leave Montpelier, the road will follow the Winooski River. To your left, you will get views of occasional high croplands. As you come into the village of East Montpelier, you will reach the junction of Routes 2 and 14. Stay to the left and take Route 14 for 1 mile and you will see the Bragg Farm Sugarhouse and Gift Shop on your left.

The Bragg family has been making maple syrup for five generations. If you visit during early spring, you are welcome to venture into the sugarhouse and watch them boil down the sap to make syrup. Adjoining the sugarhouse is the gift shop, which features Vermont specialty foods, cheeses, and, of course, maple products. Like Morse Farm, Bragg Farm makes some excellent maple creemees.

↝ Plainfield and Marshfield

We will now head into the towns of Plainfield and Marshfield, neither of which is aptly named. Plainfield is not particularly flat and Marshfield is not notably marshy. Plainfield was originally named St. Andrews, but an early landowner didn't like the name and offered to buy the town a new set of record-keeping books for the privilege of giving it a new name. He named it in honor of his hometown in Connecticut. As for Marshfield, it was named after a guy named Marsh. More appropriate names for these towns would mention their rugged hilly landscapes or perhaps the fact that the Winooski River cuts through them.

After leaving Bragg Farm, return on Route 14 to the junction of Routes 2 and 14. This time, turn left back onto Route 2 East and drive the 3 miles to Plainfield. When you reach the blinking light at the center of town, you have a couple of options. If you have resisted the urge to snack and it is now time for a sit-down meal, turn right (onto Main Street). Almost immediately on your left will be the River Run Restaurant, which serves hearty Southern fare.

Hollister Hill Farm Bed and Breakfast

To reach the last stop on the tour, and a comfortable place to sleep for the night, return to Route 2 in downtown Plainfield and continue north for less than half a mile. Turn left onto Hollister Hill Road. Follow the dirt road as it climbs and twists up the hill. After 2 miles you will reach the Hollister Hill Farm Bed and Breakfast.

Owners Bob and Lee Light farmed for years down the hill in Plainfield before buying this hilltop farm more than twenty years ago. They began as a dairy operation but found it hard to make ends meet. So they sold their herd, began raising beefalo (a cross between cattle and bison), chickens, and pigs. They also started taking guests into their 1820s farmhouse. The Lights tirelessly answer questions about farming; they see it as part of their job to educate the public about agriculture. Part of the experience is just being there, eating breakfast made with truly farm-fresh ingredients, touring the barn and maple sugarhouse, or just watching the beefalo as they meander across one of the prettiest farm settings in central Vermont.

Cabot Creamery
Cabot
800-837-4261
www.cabotcheese.com

The visitors center is open year-round: January, from 10 a.m. to 4 p.m.; February through May, 9 a.m. to 4 p.m; June through October, 9 a.m. to 5 p.m.; November and December, 9 a.m. to 4 p.m. Admission is $1. Children under 12 get in free. The Cabot Annex on Route 100 in Waterbury Center is open every day except New Year's, Easter, Thanksgiving, and Christmas, from 9 a.m. to 6 p.m.

Perennial Pleasures Nursery
East Hardwick
802-472-5104
www.perennialpleasures.net

Open 10 a.m. to 5 p.m., every day except Monday, May through September. English cream teas are served from 12 to 4 p.m. Memorial Day to Labor Day.

Vermont Daylilies
Greensboro
802-533-2438

Willey's Store
Greensboro
802-533-2621

Applecheek Farm
Hyde Park
802-888-4482
www.applecheekfarm.com

This is a working dairy farm, so please call ahead to arrange a visit.

Cady's Falls Nursery
Morrisville
802-888-5559
   Open May through October.
In May and June, from 10 a.m. to
6 p.m. Tuesday through Sunday.
In July and August, open Tuesday
through Saturday, from 10 a.m.
to 6 p.m. In September and
October, open by chance or by
appointment.

Cold Hollow Cider Mill
Waterbury Center
800-3-APPLES
www.coldhollow.com
Open seven days a week from 8
a.m. to 7 p.m. during the
summer; from 8 a.m. to 6 p.m.
during the rest of the year.

Ben & Jerry's Factory
Waterbury Center
866-BJ-TOURS
www.benjerry.com
   Open for tours October 24
through May from 10 a.m. to 6
p.m.; during June from 9 a.m. to
6 p.m.; during July through late
August from 9 a.m. to 9 p.m.;
and from late August through
late October from 9 a.m. to 7
p.m. Admission for adults is $3,
for seniors $2, and children 12
and younger get in free.

Vermont State House
Montpelier
802-223-2228
www.vtstatehouse.org
   The building is open Monday
through Saturday from 8:30 a.m.
to 4:30 p.m. Guided tours
available July through mid-
October, Monday through
Friday, 10 a.m. to 3:30 p.m.
Saturday tours are offered from
11:00 a.m. to 2:30 p.m. Group
tours must be arranged in
advance. If a tour guide is
unavailable, you may also take a
self-guided tour using a map.

Morse Farm Maple Sugarworks
Montpelier
800-242-2740
www.morsefarm.com
   Open daily from 9 a.m. to 5
p.m. During the summer from 8
a.m. to 8 p.m.

Bragg Farm
East Montpelier
800-376-5757
802-223-5757
www.braggfarm.com
   Open May through October
from 8:30 a.m. to 8 p.m.;
November through April from
8:30 a.m. to 6 p.m.

Restaurants

Finkerman's Riverside BBQ
Montpelier
802-229-2295

Open from 11 a.m. through 10 p.m., Tuesday through Sunday. Traditional Southern barbecue with touches of Creole and Southwestern cooking. Entrées range from $9 to $18.

New England Culinary Institute (NECI)
Main Street Grill & Bar
802-223-3188
Chef's Table 802-229-9202
La Brioche 802-229-0443
Montpelier
www.neci.edu/restaurants

Students at NECI learn their craft at these restaurants. The first two are elegant restaurants serving innovative cuisine, with the Chef's Table being the more formal. Menu items at the Main Street Grill range from $10 to $17. At the Chef's Table the range is $18 to $25. La Brioche is a bakery/café.

River Run Restaurant
Plainfield
802-454-1246

The River Run brings Southern-inspired cuisine to Vermont—their slogan is "Northern Hospitality, Southern Ingenuity." The restaurant serves three meals a day, Tuesday through Sunday. Breakfast items range from $3 to $10, lunch entrées cost between $5 and $11, and dinner entrées run between $11 and $18. The dinner menu for children includes breakfast.

Lodging

Hollister Hill Farm Bed and Breakfast
Marshfield
www.hollisterhillfarm.com
802-454-7725

This bed-and-breakfast offers three large double bedrooms. Two rooms have working fireplaces; the other has a sauna. Children are welcome. Rates are $85 to $100 per room per night, double occupancy; there is a charge of $20 for each extra person in a double room. A family suite is also available for $135 to $150 per night.

For more lodging options, check the extensive listings at www.vermontvacation.com or call 800-VERMONT.

Central Vermont
Southern Sector

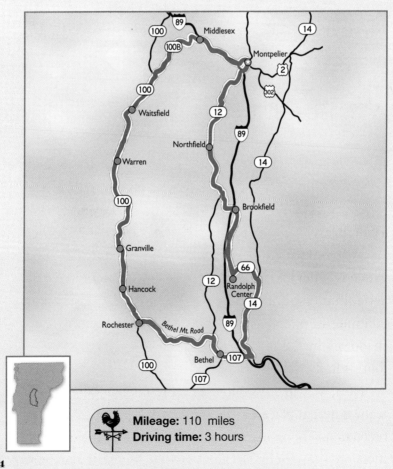

Mileage: 110 miles
Driving time: 3 hours

A Tale of Two Valleys

You can learn a lot from taking a drive. If you look around and pay attention, you can start reading the landscape like a book. This tour will take you through a pair of lovely valleys, each with its own story to tell.

First, you will head south through the Mad River Valley, which is better known for its prime skiing than for its prime agricultural land. It is easy to see why. While dairy farms continue to operate here, they are almost literally over-shadowed by the soaring peaks that draw skiers and other tourists to the valley.

Next, we will cross into the East Randolph Valley, a radically different place known for its farming, not its outdoor recreation. The farms in this valley don't face the develop-ment pressures exerted by ski resorts and tourist destinations.

⤳ Middlesex to Moretown

Start at the northern entrance to the Mad River Valley on Route 100B in Middlesex. (Alternatively, you can take Route 100 from Waterbury, which merges with Route 100B seven miles down the valley, but then you would miss the pleasant village of Moretown and some lovely stretches of the Mad River.) To reach Route 100B South, take Route 2 into Middlesex. You can't miss the junction of the two roads; the village is small.

Heading south on Route 100B, you will pass by a hydroelectric plant, which captures some of the power that gave the river its reputation for madness. Over the next 10 miles, farms dot the landscape. You will see cornfields, hay fields, and horse farms. The fields are interrupted only after about 6 miles when you reach the village of Moretown, which sits beside a somewhat wild section of the Mad River.

Just after Moretown, Route 100B merges with Route 100 which you will follow south from there.

About 3 miles below Moretown you will see a cluster of dairy farms sitting beside the road with land behind them flowing down to the Mad River. The mountains of the Green Mountain National Forest serve as the backdrop to this picturesque scene. These are also some of the few working farms in the valley.

⤳ Waitsfield and Warren

In a way, the landscape in this area works against the farms, because some of the mountains are particularly well suited to skiing. Indeed, they are home to the famous Sugarbush ski area, which like many resorts has moved heavily into real estate development. (Nearby is the much smaller and cooperatively owned Mad River Glen ski area, which enjoys a cult following, but has chosen not to develop condominiums and other amenities.)

Sugarbush's popularity has brought vitality to the valley, but it has also caused land prices to rise, making farming a less affordable option. For more than twenty years, local residents have been working hard to preserve their valley. Their successes are due largely to the efforts of a unique partnership consisting of an environmental group, town officials, and members of the local business community. Together, they have succeeded in conserving large swaths of valley farmland and have prevented the rampant development seen near so many other ski areas. So the Mad River Valley has managed to hold on to its dairy farming heritage during an era when skiing is the local cash cow.

Joining the valley's dairy farms are a growing number of horse farms. Many of these equestrian enterprises are what some would call "hobby farms"—they survive because their owners don't need to make a living from them. They might not contribute as much to Vermont's farming economy as working farms do, but they do serve a valuable function in keeping land open.

Mad River Path

If you want to explore some of the open land we've been talking about, consider a walk or ride down the Mad River Path, a 6-mile-long nature trail that you can pick up in Waitsfield. The easiest place to find the trail is at the junction of Route 100 and Meadow Road, which is about midway between Moretown and Waitsfield. Heading south on Route 100, you will see the trailhead on the left shortly after the sign for Small Dog Electronics.

The trail, which is open year-round except during the fall hunting season, is accessible by foot or mountain bike, as well as by ski or snowmobile in the winter. Following the natural contours of the land, the trail passes through the area's historic farming district and offers stunning views of the mountains and valley.

Kenyon's

Just before you enter Waitsfield, which is 5 miles south of Moretown on Route 100, on your left you will see a cornerstone of the local

Vermont Fresh Network

Poet and farmer Wendell Berry once commented that "eating is an agricultural act." He's right, of course. Eating is the last stage of a transaction that starts with the farmer.

The folks with the Vermont Fresh Network understand the connection between the people who grow and raise food and the people who eat it. They've taken on the job of trying to nurture those links and create new ones. The heart of the operation is the organization's Web site (www.vermontfresh.net), which acts as a sort of virtual dating service for hundreds of vegetable and fruit gardeners, meat producers, cheesemakers, dairies, restaurateurs, and food stores. By letting everyone know who else is out there, and what kind of food they deal in, the Network hopes to create collaborations all along Vermont's food chain.

The Network wants to make it easy for consumers to buy good, fresh local food across Vermont. When you buy local food you help keep farmers in business.

If you want to know whether a restaurant is a member of the Network, look for a Vermont Fresh Network sticker in the window or a note on the menu. By the way, almost all the restaurants recommended in this guidebook are members.

farming community: Kenyon's, a country farm store, offering farming supplies as well as pet and gardening supplies, home improvement items, and clothing. You can pick up fishing licenses here or even join the Vermont Association of Snow Travelers, a statewide snowmobiling club.

After you pass through Waitsfield, you will notice the valley begin to narrow and farmland give way to a slender river valley. Five miles down the road is the picturesque village of Warren, which is worth a stop. As you approach the town, you'll see a sign for it, steering you left off Route 100 onto Main Street. After a quarter mile, you will be in the middle of the village.

The Warren Store

Tucked beside a stream, the Warren Store attracts both locals and visitors, who come for the deli sandwiches, salads, and pastries that are served in the back. The store also stocks a nice selection of snack food, wine, and gourmet items. Upstairs is a store carrying an eclectic and stylish mix of jewelry, clothing, and household items. The back room features campy toys and gag gifts. If you are grabbing lunch at the store on a warm day, it's nice to sit on the deck, which perches over a waterfall.

When you leave Warren, continue on the road through town. In a mile it will hook up with Route 100 again. Turn left to continue south to Granville and Rochester, where you'll visit a place that produces wooden bowls and clapboards using nineteenth-century techniques, as well as a traditional dairy farm that also serves as a bed-and-breakfast.

⌁ Granville

As you travel along Route 100, look around. You'll notice that the valley you've been driving through has narrowed dramatically. The open views of the northern end of the valley have been replaced with a winding trail through the forested Granville Gulch. And with the views have gone the farms. The gulch is too tight to farm, but it is good for logging.

The woods to your right are part of the Green Mountain National Forest, and the harvesting of trees here helps support local loggers and mill owners. You'll see an example of the family-owned mills just ahead in Granville. But first, as the gulch gets particularly narrow, keep an eye out for Moss Glen Falls, a spectacular waterfall that cascades down from Roosevelt Mountain. You'll see it on the right, about 7 miles south of Warren. If you want to explore, there is a small parking area on the right side of the road.

The Bowl Mill

Two miles south of the falls, you'll enter the settled portion of Granville. As Route 100 curves to the left, you'll see a sign for The Bowl Mill. The sign is small and unassuming, much like the mill. "Small and unassuming" have worked for about 150 years.

Since 1857, the mill has turned out one-piece bowls. Today, most wooden bowls on the market are made from multiple pieces of wood. The factory is a time capsule of sorts. Workers still use the same equipment and techniques perfected in the nineteenth century. The mill has been owned by a succession of four families during its history. Similarly, some families have provided generations of workers for the mill, which also continues to manufacture clapboards the old-fashioned way. It is hard to argue that the mill should alter its practices. If something works, why change it?

The only significant modification to the mill is that it is no longer water-powered. When the flood of 1927 washed away the Granville Dam, the owners thought it was time to switch to electricity.

Guided tours to the mill are not offered, but you are welcome to poke around on your own. Workers are used to people stopping by and are happy to answer questions. If you want to tour the factory, get there between 9 a.m. and 3 p.m. or you'll miss the workers, whose shift starts at 6 a.m. Adjacent to the two factory buildings is the company's store. There you will find all sizes of bowls cut from such woods as hard maple, yellow birch, black cherry, and beech.

↷ Rochester

Our next destination is Liberty Hill Farm in Rochester, a working dairy farm and country inn. To reach Rochester, continue south on Route 100. Four miles after leaving The Bowl Mill, the road will take you through the town of Hancock, named for John Hancock, the American patriot with the famous signature. All but this corner of the town lies to your right, within the Green Mountain National Forest.

Another 4 miles down the road, you'll come upon Rochester. With a population of about 1,200, it is about three times larger than Hancock. But like its neighbor to the north, much of the town is national forest land. Vermont verde antique marble is quarried in town. We'll be stopping at one of the few dairy farms in the area.

Liberty Hill Farm

If you want to see how a real dairy farm operates, staying here is one of your best bets. To reach the farm, drive 3 miles south of Rochester village on Route 100, turn right onto Liberty Hill Road, cross the bridge, and turn left toward the red barn.

Liberty Hill Farm has been in operation since 1787. The beautiful white farmhouse, which contains seven guest rooms, is 150 years old. The hosts are Bob and Beth Kennett, who invite guests to visit the barn, feed the calves, swim in the adjacent river, or just read a book on the porch. The mood is relaxed and homey. Liberty Hill Farm is technically a bed-and-breakfast-and-dinner. Meals are served family-style at a large dining-room table.

↝ Royalton

Next we will cross the height between Rochester Mountain and Bethel Mountain, pass quickly down the valley that contains Randolph (to the north), and proceed into the East Randolph Valley (it's easier than it sounds). Our tour will stop at a vegetable farm that welcomes visitors and overnight guests who like to camp.

First, from Liberty Hill Farm backtrack the 3 miles to the center of Rochester and turn right just before the Mobil station onto the Bethel Mountain Road. The town's green will be on your right. It is a lovely spot for a picnic or perhaps a game of Frisbee. Follow this road out of town. It will begin to climb gradually. At 1.3 miles, turn right to stay on Bethel Mountain Road and stay on it for the next 8 miles as it snakes through the hills. The area may seem remote, but there are signs that suggest it was once farmed. For example, at one point, about 6 miles after you turn onto Bethel Mountain Road, you will see a row of large, stately maples running along a battered old stone wall.

Eaton's Sugarhouse

When you come down the mountain, you will meet Route 12. Turn right and head south. In a mile you will reach the center of Bethel. The road will "T." Stay to the left and follow the signs for Route 107 East. After 3 miles you'll pass under Interstate 89. Just ahead, at the junction of Routes 107 and 14 in North Royalton, you will see Eaton's Sugarhouse, a longtime institution in the area.

The building has sections that date back to just after the Civil War, when apple cider was made there. Cider is still produced on the premises, but the business has expanded considerably since then to include, as the name suggests, a maple sugarhouse as well as a gift shop. Since 1967, however, Eaton's has been best known perhaps for its popular restaurant, which serves breakfast and lunch. The breakfast menu is served all day, and the pancakes have a loyal following.

Four Springs Farm

Another Royalton business hoping to become a local favorite is Four Springs Farm, a multipurpose place that not only sells produce, but also offers camping and treasure hunts. To reach the farm, turn right out of Eaton's parking lot and head north on Route 14 for about 3 miles, then turn right onto Post Farm Road. Follow this road uphill for about a mile until it ends at a T intersection with Gee Hill Road. Turn left on Gee Hill Road. Four Springs Farm is just ahead on the left. Park at the top of the farm driveway if you plan to start with the Valley Quest (see page 83).

Jinny Cleland bought the property in 2001 and has been running it as a CSA (Community Supported Agriculture) operation, which is a system in which community members subscribe to a portion of a season's harvest and then pick up the produce directly from the farmer. The arrangement gives people direct access to locally grown produce and saves the farmer hours of work to market the harvest.

Cleland has found another way to share her 70-acre farm — opening it up for camping. The campground includes a simple wooden cabin with four bunks and a number of secluded tent sites tucked beside fields and orchards. Each site has a tent platform, fireplace, and picnic table. All campers have access to the wash house, a building equipped with toilets, sinks, and showers.

Yet another attraction at Four Springs Farm is the Valley Quest treasure hunt. Participants roam around the property carrying maps and searching for riddle-like clues. The quests lead visitors to hidden special places and teach about the region's natural and cultural history. If you plan to do the quest at Four Springs Farm, be sure to visit the farm's Web site first (See Lodging, page 89).

Valley Quest treasure hunts have been arranged in 50 towns in the Connecticut River Valley. So far, more than 150 quests have been created by local community members.

↷ Randolph

From Royalton we will drive through the classic dairying country of the East Randolph Valley. To reach our next destination, a dairy farm that makes its own cheese, upon leaving Four Springs Farm, return down Post Farm Road to Route 14. Turn right, and continue north on Route 14. The road follows the Second Branch of the White River as it cuts through this landscape of barns and fields. After 5 miles, you will reach the beautiful small farming town of East Randolph. Turn left onto Route 66 and follow it for 3.6 miles, until you see Ridge Road on your right. Turn right and follow Ridge Road for 1.4 miles

Cow Breeds

Not all Vermont cows are black and white. Perhaps Ben & Jerry's is to blame for the misconception. The makers of the popular ice cream put images of black and white cows seemingly everywhere—on their containers, t-shirts, mugs, trucks. These cows are **Holsteins**, or technically Holstein-Freisians, brought here in the 1850s from the Netherlands and Germany, because of their ability to produce a lot of milk. Holsteins produce an average of 55 pounds, or 6.4 gallons, of milk a day. That's why farmers like them. Although Holsteins *are* a common sight in Vermont, they have a lot of company.

Jerseys landed here from the British isle of Jersey around the same time as the Holsteins. These brown cows produce about 39 pounds, or 4.5 gallons, of milk per day. That amount might pale next to the Holstein, but the Jersey produces the highest ratio of milk to body weight. While Holsteins weigh in at about 1,500 pounds, Jerseys are a relatively slight 900 pounds. That favorable ratio is the reason they are the second most popular breed in the state.

Brown Swiss arrived from Switzerland in about 1870. Their milk has a high butterfat content, making it ideal for processing into products such as butter and cheese. Brown Swiss actually vary from silver to dark brown. They produce 46 pounds, or 5.3 gallons, of milk per day. They weigh about 1,300 pounds.

Guernseys, which are orangey-red, often with white legs, also produce rich milk. They came from a British isle, Guernsey, in the 1840s. Guernseys produce 39 pounds, or 4.6 gallons, of milk daily and weigh a modest 1,100 pounds.

Ayrshires arrived here from Scotland in the 1820s. They were particularly adept at walking in rocky terrain and adapted to the cold climate. These rusty red-and-white cows weigh about 1,200 pounds and produce 43 pounds, or 5 gallons of milk, a day.

and then turn right onto North Randolph Road. In 1.5 miles you will reach a four-corner intersection. Neighborly Farms is on the left.

Neighborly Farms of Vermont

When Rob and Linda Dimmick took over Rob's family's dairy farm, they decided the business would be more profitable if they became cheesemakers, instead of relying solely on selling their cows' milk at wholesale prices. Thus was born the Neighborly Farms of Vermont line of cheeses. Today, Neighborly Farms makes feta, Monterey Jack, Colby, and several varieties of cheddar. The Dimmicks produce all their milk organically, so they can sell their cheese at a premium to consumers interested in organic products.

The couple made another decision along the way. They wanted to open their farm to visitors so people wouldn't lose the knowledge of how their food is made. The Dimmicks have redesigned the barn so that visitors can watch the cheese being made through a large window. Cheesemaking takes place Monday, Wednesday, and Friday.

❧ Brookfield to Montpelier

Next, we'll head toward Montpelier, with a couple of stops along the way. First up is the town of Brookfield. From Neighborly Farms, go back down North Randolph Road to Ridge Road. Turn right and head north. Since the road follows the ridgeline, on your left you will see beautiful glimpses of the Green Mountains to the west. Follow Ridge Road for 5 miles, until it ends next to a church. Turn left. You are in Brookfield.

The Floating Bridge

Just ahead on your left you will see a local landmark, the Floating Bridge. Just as the name suggests, the bridge really does float. The 320-foot span rests on plastic barrels, which is surely not how it was floated when the bridge was first built in 1820. The bridge you see today is the seventh incarnation of the bridge. The original one was built by townspeople after a local man drowned while trying to cross thin ice. The construction of the span is such that several inches of water often sit in the one travel lane, enough to occasionally splash pedestrians, but not enough to flood your engine.

Ariel's Restaurant

If you happen to be in Brookfield around dinnertime, consider stopping in at Ariel's Restaurant. To find it, instead of turning left across the bridge, continue straight. The restaurant is the first house on the left. Ariel's serves dinner five nights a week (Wednesday through Sunday), but is closed for the months of April and November. The menu features multicultural fare prepared using fresh, local ingredients. The restaurant is known for its carefully selected wine list and its excellent desserts.

If you would rather prepare your own meal, stop by one of Vermont's farmers' markets. We'll head to a local favorite next.

Ellie's Farm Market and Gift Shop

To reach Ellie's, follow Route 65 West across the Floating Bridge and out of town. Route 65 is a dirt road here, but it is well marked. The road takes you past Allis State Park on your left (there's a wonderful view from the park's fire tower), and in 3 miles you will reach the junction with Route 12. Turn right to follow Route 12 North. This road takes you through the town of East Roxbury and, after 6 miles, you will come to the town of Northfield. Just north of Northfield, you will enter Riverton, a village in the town of Berlin, and home of Ellie's, which you will see on your right.

Ellie's Farm Market and Gift Shop traces its roots back to 1948, when founders Ella and Bill Moynihan started selling extra vegetables from their large garden to neighbors. The Moynihans' son Bill and his wife, Karen, now run the business, which has grown considerably since those early days. Now Ellie's sells all manner of fruits and vegetables the Moynihans grow themselves. They also sell starter plants in the spring and freshly pressed apple cider in the fall. In the gift shop, they stock everything from candles to syrup to Cabot cheddar cheese.

Ellie's is perhaps best known for its carved pumpkin displays set up each year just before Halloween. Hundreds of pumpkins—some carved with delicate designs, others with humorous caricatures and word plays—line the hillside beside the store. Once, a local man asked Karen to carve a marriage proposal in pumpkins. Karen said yes, as did the man's girlfriend.

We now continue on to Montpelier, where we'll visit the Vermont Historical Society, whose exhibits include a look at the state's agricultural past.

Vermont Historical Society Museum

To reach the museum, continue north on Route 12. In just under 7 miles, Route 12 will take you down a steep hill, and in front of you there will be a view of the state capitol. At the first light continue going straight, crossing the bridge into downtown Montpelier. Turn left at the second light, onto State Street. Continue straight for two blocks. Then, immediately on your right, you will see a large brick building with a white railing around the porch. This is the Pavilion Building, which houses some state government offices and the Vermont Historical Society Museum.

Inside, you will discover the society's recently opened permanent exhibit, which offers a chronological view of the state's history. Interspersed within the exhibit, which examines everything from the pre-colonial lives of Native Americans to the development of the ski industry, you will find an exploration of the changing use of land in Vermont. You'll learn about the ebbs and flows of agriculture, from the rise of the sheep craze in the early 1800s to its collapse in mid-century, which was followed by the rise of dairy farming and the transformation of the state into a dairy economy.

The exhibit helps provide context for what we have already seen on this tour of two strikingly different valleys: one where farmers are adapting to changes brought on by the influx of tourists in general and skiers in particular; the other where farmers are continuing to farm more or less as their families have for generations. Leave yourself 45 minutes to an hour and a half to visit.

Mad River Path

Waitsfield

www.madriverpath.org

For a map of the path, check the Web site.

Kenyon's

Waitsfield

802-496-3922

Open 7 a.m. to 7 p.m. weekdays; 7 a.m. to 5 p.m. weekends.

The Warren Store

Warren

802-496-3864

Open Monday through Saturday 8 a.m. to 7 p.m.; Sunday 8 a.m. to 6 p.m.

The Bowl Mill

Granville

800-828-1005

www.bowlmill.com

Open weekdays 9 a.m. to 5 p.m.; factory tours start at 7 a.m. and run only until 3 p.m.

Eaton's Sugarhouse

Royalton

802-763-8809

888-886-2753

www.vtmaple.com

Open 7 a.m. to 3 p.m. daily.

Neighborly Farms
of Vermont

Randolph

802-728-4700

888-212-6898

Open 9 a.m. to 5 p.m. Monday through Saturday. Call ahead for special events and a cheesemaking schedule.

Ellie's Farm Market
and Gift Shop

Riverton

802-485-7968

Open daily 8:30 a.m. to 6 p.m. Closing times are later during spring, foliage season, and before Christmas.

Vermont Historical Society
Museum

Montpelier

802-828-2291

www.vermonthistory.org

Open Tuesday through Saturday 10 a.m. to 4 p.m. year-round; May through October it is also open on Sunday from 12 to 4 p.m. Admission is $12 for families, $5 for adults, $3 for children and seniors, and free for children under 6.

Restaurants

American Flatbread
Waitsfield
www.americanflatbread.com
802-496-8856

Serves dinner (pizzas and salads only) from 5:30 to 9:30 p.m. Friday and Saturday. A wood-fired oven serves as a centerpiece for the informal restaurant. No reservations, but starting at 4:30 p.m. you can come in person to put your name on the waiting list.

Pitcher Inn
Warren
www.pitcherinn.com
802-496-6350

Open for dinner every day except Tuesday from 6 to 9:30 p.m. Features new American cuisine and an award-winning wine list; Entrées range from $22 to $36.

Ariel's Restaurant & Pond Village Pub
Brookfield
www.arielsrestaurant.com
802-276-3939

Open Wednesday through Sunday for dinner. Call for hours. Pub entrées range from $11 to $13; restaurant entrées range from $20 to $26.

Sarducci's
Montpelier
www.central-vt.com/web/sarducci
802-223-0229

Open daily for lunch and dinner. Italian cuisine served up in generous portions. Lunch entrées range from $6 to $8; dinner entrées range from $9 to $17.

Lodging

Liberty Hill Farm
Rochester
802-767-3926
www.libertyhillfarm.com

Nightly rates, which include dinner and a full breakfast, are $75 per adult, $55 per teenager, and $35 per child 12 and under.

Four Springs Farm
Royalton
www.fourspringsfarm.com
802-763-7296

This working vegetable farm offers walk-in tent sites and a cabin. Costs vary depending on the time of year. Tent sites cost roughly $20 a night, and the cabin costs about $60.

For more lodging options, check the extensive listings at www.vermontvacation.com or call 800-VERMONT.

The Champlain Valley
Burlington Area

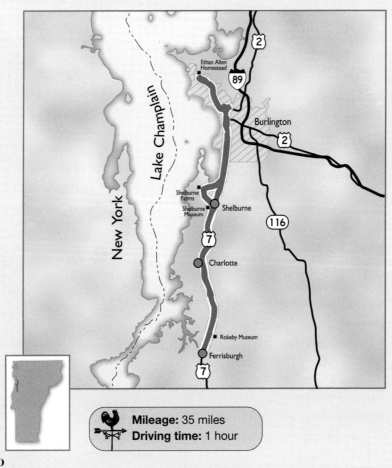

Mileage: 35 miles
Driving time: 1 hour

90

Farming Near the Smallest Big City in America

The Burlington area is an anomaly in Vermont. It is densely populated and urban—at least by Vermont standards. Roughly a quarter of the state's population of 600,000 is clustered around Burlington, the county's hub and the state's largest city.

Vermonters who don't care for the area's urban and suburban aspects like to quip about Chittenden County: "It's not Vermont, but you can see Vermont from there." Indeed, the area is grappling like no other part of the state with the forces of sprawling development that have made much of the rest of the country seem generic. Still, many parts of the county remain open and offer stunning views of

Lake Champlain and the Adirondack Mountains of New York. Many of those undeveloped areas are no accident. Often they are the result of efforts by conservation groups to keep land open, and by agriculturalists to keep it working (see page 101).

People might quibble over whether Chittenden County feels like the rest of Vermont, but there is no debating that it is a great place to see the state, in the sense that it contains some of the best-preserved examples of Vermont's agricultural past. This tour will take you to three museums and a working farm/environmental education center that will give you a glimpse of the farming heritage that, along with Burlington's then-bustling harbor, brought wealth to this part of Vermont during the nineteenth and early twentieth centuries. Along the way, we'll also stop at a berry farm and get a chance to take a short hike. Continuing our theme of farm museums, we'll slip into Addison County to visit two historic farms in Ferrisburgh.

If you want to visit all or most of the sites on this tour, you could spend two or three days here. These stops don't lend themselves to quick, drive-by visits. These are places where you will want to linger.

↩ Burlington

Burlington has long been the largest community in Vermont. People are drawn here because of its active cultural scene, numerous fine restaurants, lively pedestrian shopping area, and commanding view of the lake.

People were originally drawn to settle here because of the sheltered harbor and the nearby rivers that provided water power to mills. People also came here to farm, and still do. Burlington's northern end is capped by the Intervale, a large expanse of particularly fertile land at the delta of the Winooski River. That's where we are heading next.

The Intervale

The Intervale area of Burlington is proof that agriculture and urban areas can coexist. What you need is great soil and a group of talented people who are committed to farming. Today that combination has made the Intervale fertile ground for agricultural innovation.

For a time, farming in the Intervale, which dates back roughly 500 years, seemed doomed. By 1960,this section of rich Winooski River floodplain had become a neglected backwater. Farming operations were dwindling and the city was using the area as a dump. But in the 1980s, visionary community members began to restore the area to its place of agricultural prominence. Will Raap, one of the leaders, established the Gardener's Supply retail company there in 1983. The same year, the McNeil Generating Station was built. Fueled by woodchips, the station is New England's largest renewable energy power plant. Soon after, a local junkyard was closed and cleaned up, and creative agricultural businesses flocked to the area.

Today, the nonprofit Intervale Foundation runs a network of sustainable agricultural ventures that produce everything from food to fiber to fuel. Gardener's Supply is currently the main attraction for visitors, though locals regularly visit the Intervale to buy fresh produce or to drop off yard or kitchen waste at the area's compost operation.

In 2007, construction will begin on the Intervale Public Market, which is modeled after an old-style European public market. There, visitors will be able to buy locally produced organic and specialty foods, including tofu, bread, beer, ice cream, and chocolates.

To reach the Intervale, drive west on Route 2 (Williston Road, which becomes Main Street) toward downtown Burlington. Just past the University of Vermont green, take a right onto South Prospect Street. Follow Prospect Street past the green, through a residential area and down a steep hill until you reach a traffic light. Continue straight. Prospect Street becomes Intervale Road. Cross the railroad tracks. Just ahead is the Gardener's Supply Company. Park here and walk or follow the road a short distance to the other businesses that are growing in Burlington's Intervale.

Ethan Allen Homestead & Museum

The Ethan Allen Homestead Museum was created long after its most famous inhabitant exited the scene. The homestead was opened to the public in 1989, exactly 200 years after the patriot Ethan Allen died here shortly after returning across the lake on a horse-drawn sleigh.

Getting to the homestead is not easy. But at least it is unlikely to be as perilous as Ethan's final trip. To reach the homestead, start on Pearl Street in downtown Burlington. It is the street that borders the north end of the Church Street pedestrian mall. Follow Pearl Street west (toward the lake). Pearl Street will end at a traffic light at the intersection with Battery Street. Turn right at the light and then left at the next light onto Sherman Street for 1 block, then bear right onto North Avenue. Then take your third right onto Ward Street. At the end of the street, turn right at the stop sign onto Manhattan Drive. At the light one block ahead turn left onto Route 127. You will take the first exit off Route 127, marked "North Ave." Partway along the looping exit ramp you will see a small sign for the Ethan Allen Homestead. Turn right. The road will take you straight to the museum.

Ethan Allen, leader of the Green Mountain Boys and head of the force that took Fort Ticonderoga during the Revolutionary War, moved to the area around the homestead in 1787 to farm.

In the years after his death, the farm changed hands several times. People eventually lost track of where the farm had been. Then in the 1970s a local historian announced that he had discovered the homestead, which he said had been hidden by a succession of renovations and additions. Today the restored farmhouse sits adjacent to what is still active farmland. Exhibits at the homestead museum discuss the land Ethan and his wife, Fanny, owned and how they and others worked it over time.

You can take a guided tour of the restored home and walk along the nature trails that wind through the property. Displays at the homestead highlight the domestic life of farmers at that time. The museum has a gift shop that sells books, toys, and other items connected with the era.

If you visit the homestead, take a moment to consider this: Ethan Allen owned great swaths of Vermont farmland, yet he chose this area for his homestead.

From here, we will head south to the town of Shelburne, and two of Vermont's best-known attractions.

To reach Shelburne from the Ethan Allen Homestead, return to Route 127, turning right from the museum road onto that route and heading back toward Burlington. At the traffic light, turn left onto North Avenue and follow it for 1.5 miles, bear left onto Sherman Street, then turn right onto Battery Street at the light. Drive to the bottom of the hill to the light at Main Street. Turn left onto Main Street and drive up this hill for 3 blocks, then turn right onto St. Paul Street (which becomes Route 7 after about a mile). Follow Route 7 South. About 4 miles south of Main Street, you will pass the junction of Route 7 and Interstate 189 (which is really just the access road to Interstate 89). Continue south on Route 7.

↜ Shelburne

Three things have contributed to the feel of the town of Shelburne—one natural, two human creations. The natural feature is Lake Champlain, which flits in and out of view as you approach Shelburne along Route 7. The town enjoys a long stretch of the lake shoreline marked by numerous bays and points. The lake, which affords sweeping views of the Adirondack Mountains, helps form people's attachment to this part of Vermont.

The town is also home to a pair of exquisite rural showplaces: a museum with a mind-bogglingly thorough collection of items of early American life—it's been called "a thinking person's theme park"—and a beautiful working farm and education center dedicated to demonstrating sustainable agricultural practices.

We'll visit the farm first.

Shelburne Farms

Shelburne Farms is located just west of the center of Shelburne Village. Three miles south of the Route 7/Interstate 189 intersection, you will reach Bay Road at a traffic light. Turn right here and follow Bay Road for just under 2 miles, until it brings you to the gates of the farm. Ask at the gate how to catch the shuttle that takes visitors to the heart of the property. (Note: Although Route 7 is the most direct route, there can be a lot of traffic. If you would like a less traveled approach to Shelburne from Burlington, Spear Street runs parallel to Route 7. Consult your map for specifics.)

Dr. William Seward Webb and his wife, Lila Vanderbilt Webb, wanted to use their great wealth for a noble purpose: creating a model estate farm. Starting in 1886, they bought up small farms along Lake Champlain south of Burlington. The result was Shelburne Farms, which at one point encompassed 3,800 acres. Today it is a spectacular 1,400-acre working farm that is still directed by a member of the Webb family. The farm's mission is to educate the public by using the land—whether it is for making cheese, growing grain, or managing the forest—in ways that are environmentally, economically, and culturally sustainable.

For the sake of the farm's tranquility, visitors are asked to park at the entrance. There they can visit the extensive gift shop, which features the farm's cheese and other Vermont-made products, before heading on to the farm. You can reach the farm in two ways: either by foot, along some of the property's 7 miles of trails, or by riding a

Monitor Barns

Anyone who believes that ingenuity is a modern phenomenon ought to visit the Richmond Monitor Barn Project located 2 miles east of Richmond village on Route 2 (about 25 minutes from downtown Burlington).

The twin, four-story structures stand as testament to the inventiveness that agriculture brings out in farmers. Built around 1900, the barns contain several innovations that made them models of efficiency. By building their barns backed into the hillside, farmers could install a "high-drive" ramp to the top floor. They would then drive their hay wagons into the top story of the barn, where the hay was stored in bays. To feed the cows, they would drop the hay into the cows' mangers on the second floor. When it was time to muck out the cows' manure, the farmers shoveled the stuff through trap doors to the ground floor and into wagons, which transported the nutrient-rich manure back to the fields to be used as fertilizer.

The barns were healthier for cows, since they featured monitor-roofs, which allow for better ventilation. Where the roofs of standard barns would normally peak, a monitor barn has something resembling a long, low shed with a peaked roof and windows running the length of the structure.

The Richmond Land Trust and the Vermont Youth Conservation Corps have extensively reconstructed the west monitor barn in Richmond. Renovations are also planned for the east barn. The west barn is open occasionally to the public and is available to rent for functions.

Check the conservation corps' Web site (www.vycc.org) or call 802-241-3699 for details.

tractor-pulled wagon. Either way, you'll pass through a landscape designed by Frederick Law Olmsted, the father of American landscape architecture and designer of New York's Central Park and Boston's Emerald Necklace. As you tour the property, each new vista seems to reveal another architectural marvel or jaw-dropping view of the lake. The farm's barns are immense and ornate, matching the Webbs' dreams. The buildings are so fanciful and ambitious they have almost a dreamlike quality to them.

So, too, does the house the Webbs built, which overlooks Lake Champlain. In typical Victorian style, it was often referred to as a "summer cottage," but it is, in everything but name, a mansion. The house has been reborn as the Inn at Shelburne Farms, which manages to maintain its graciousness without seeming stuffy. The inn has 24 guest rooms, as well as a pair of cottages that can be rented. In addition, the inn's elegant restaurant serves breakfast, Sunday brunch, and dinner made with local ingredients, many of them produced on the farm. The restaurant is open to the public.

Shelburne Farms is open daily from mid-May through mid-October. A day pass entitles you to walk the trails and visit the Farm Yard and Farm Barn. The Farm Yard is a treat for animal lovers. Though you can pat the animals, this is much more than a petting zoo. Children and others are invited to get a hands-on experience, helping with chores, whether it is collecting eggs, walking a goat, milking cows, or making butter.

The barn contains the farm's award-winning cheesemaking operation. The farm makes cheese daily from May through October and tastings are available. You can also buy a loaf of the farm's organic bread as well as farm-grown vegetables. The barn contains an independent furniture maker who works only with sustainably harvested woods, most of the wood harvested from the property. Tours of the other buildings are available regularly (see Details at the end of this chapter).

From late fall through early spring, although many of its operations are closed, the farm still offers special events celebrating the seasons, such as the springtime maple syrup day and the winterfest. The farm's walking trails are open year-round.

Shelburne Museum

Shelburne is home to another gem. Like Shelburne Farms, the Shelburne Museum has strong ties to the Webb family. To reach it, turn right out of the Shelburne Farms parking area onto Harbor Road and follow it to Shelburne Village. Turn right at the light onto Route 7 South. The museum grounds begin almost immediately on your right. The entrance is at the top of the hill, .7 mile ahead on the right.

The museum was the creation of Electra Havemeyer Webb, who was married to the son of William and Lila Webb, the farm's founders. Electra was the daughter of renowned collectors of European and American paintings. She had her own passion for collecting, but she wasn't so interested in the "fine arts." She was more taken by folk art and the decorative arts—furniture, quilts, rugs, pottery, pewter—the things that make a house a home. Webb saw the beauty in objects that others viewed solely for their utility.

In 1947, she opened the Shelburne Museum in the center of the village where she and her husband had a vacation home. The museum's 45 acres are dotted with an assortment of 39 buildings that Webb had dismantled and brought to the site. Among them are an 1840 meeting house that originally stood in nearby Charlotte, an 1890 jail from the town of Castleton, and a 1780s home from the town of Cavendish. The museum is also home to a locomotive and train station, a luxury steamship, a lighthouse, and other preposterously large exhibits.

The state's farming heritage is well represented at the museum. You will find everything from a large Shaker-style round barn to a settler's log cabin to an early saltbox home to an elaborate horseshoe barn. The grounds also feature other buildings—a meeting house, a sawmill, a smokehouse, a farm shed—that were part of the rural landscape during the eighteenth and nineteenth centuries.

We are about to head south on Route 7, but if you are hungry consider a stop at **Harrington's.** The store is located across from the museum's grounds, just north of the museum entrance, on the right. Harrington's is best known for its hams, turkeys, maple syrup, and other Vermont specialty food products, but also serves pastries and coffee in the morning, and soups and sandwiches the rest of the day.

↜ Charlotte and Ferrisburgh

After leaving the Shelburne Museum we will continue south on Route 7 through Charlotte to Ferrisburgh, home of the Rokeby Museum, a preserved eighteenth-century Vermont farmstead, which served for a time as a stop on the Underground Railroad. We will pass through some of the state's best farmland. Some of it has been bought up for homes, because the area has commanding views of the Adirondacks and Lake Champlain.

Home building tends to drive up real estate prices and creates development pressure that is hard for farmers to resist. Along this stretch, however, much of the land remains agricultural, which is due in part to the work of land trusts. Land trusts use private funds to buy development rights from farmers, essentially paying farmers to keep land in operation, rather than subdividing it and selling it for house lots. Without such agreements, the views you enjoy as you drive down Route 7, and many other roads in Vermont, would look quite different. Thanks to conservation efforts, much of the scenery you'll see is farm fields and occasional long views of the lake and mountains beyond.

Charlotte Park and Wildlife Refuge

If you want to take a short hike and take in some of those views, consider a walk in the Charlotte Park and Wildlife Refuge just ahead. Five and a half miles south of the Shelburne Museum on Route 7 you'll come to a traffic light. Turn right onto Ferry Road and drive

Vermont Land Trust

If you are enjoying the view in Vermont, you might have a land trust to thank. Collectively, land trusts have preserved hundreds of thousands of acres in Vermont. Land trusts are private organizations that raise money to buy development rights from landowners.

Land trusts are particularly helpful for farmers who want to keep their land agricultural, but who are facing heavy economic pressures. One of these pressures is the pressure to develop. When they are strapped for cash, or when older farmers want to retire but can't find another farmer to buy their land, who can blame them for selling to the top bidder? The problem is that too often the buyer will be subdividing the land and putting houses on it or using the land for commercial space, taking prime agricultural land away forever and breaking up the Vermont landscape.

Land trusts help alleviate that pressure. In buying development rights from farmers and owners of other key parcels, land trusts are paying landowners a fee never to sell their land for development. It is a true win-win situation: the farmer gets a sizeable amount of money to help run the farm, and the land stays open. Farmers actually benefit twice. Since they have waived their right to development, they see their property tax bills go down. Instead of being taxed based on the land's potential development value, they are assessed based on its true value as a farm.

Vermont has many local and regional land trusts. It also has one large statewide organization, the Vermont Land Trust, which serves as a model for such groups across the country. To date, the Vermont Land Trust has protected over 430,000 acres, including more than 400 farms.

(To learn more about the Vermont Land Trust, visit its Web site at www.vlt.org or call 800-639-1709.)

about a quarter mile to the center of Charlotte Village. Turn right at the stop sign onto Greenbush Road. In less than 1 mile, you will see a parking area on your right just before you reach the railroad overpass. A short trail from the parking area heads gradually uphill. You will be walking through a 209-acre parcel recently donated to the town by the Demeter Foundation, a land conservation group founded by longtime Middlebury College professor Steven Rockefeller. The view from the top of the rise is stunning, taking in a sweeping view of the lake and the surrounding lands that lead down to it.

Charlotte Berry Farm

From the wildlife refuge return to Route 7 and continue south. In .5 mile you'll reach Charlotte Berry Farm on your right. The farm is owned by Clark and Suzanne Hinsdale, a prominent local farm family. From late June through Halloween, the Hinsdales offer a rotating array of fruits for picking. Depending on the time of year and weather conditions, you might find pick-your-own strawberries, raspberries, blueberries, or pumpkins.

Mt. Philo State Park

A mile past the berry farm you'll have a chance to take in a panoramic view of the area. Take a left onto State Park Road, which takes you quickly to the highest bit of land around. Although it has an elevation just shy of 1,000 feet, Mt. Philo offers an excellent vantage point from which to see the lowlands of the Champlain Valley sweep gracefully toward the lake with the Adirondacks providing a stunning background. You can drive the steep, narrow road to the summit or climb on your own two feet, which should take you about half an hour.

At the top, you'll find places to picnic, including an enclosed picnic shelter that is available for groups. The park, the state's oldest, also offers camping, with 10 tent sites.

Dakin Farm

Once back on Route 7, continue south to Ferrisburgh. On your right in 2.5 miles south of State Park Road, you'll see Dakin Farm, which is one of the leading purveyors of traditional Vermont foods, including maple syrup, cheddar cheeses, and smoked hams. Although the company now sells its foods at this store and another outlet in South Burlington, as well as via the internet, the family that started the business traces its roots in the area back to this farm, which dates back to the eighteenth century. Forty years ago, the Cutting family bought the old Dakin Farm and is now in its third generation of ownership. By the way, the orginal Dakins built the farmhouse that we'll visit next.

Rokeby Museum

Continue south on Route 7 and after 1.4 miles you will come to the Rokeby Museum on your left.

The museum offers visitors a unique perspective on the range of agriculture that has been practiced in Vermont. During its years as a working farm, Rokeby saw operations steadily evolve in a way that mirrored trends in the rest of the state. What started as a sheep farm became a dairy farm and finally evolved into a fruit farm.

The Rokeby Museum sprawls over 90 acres of fields and woodlands. Fortunately, if you are not up for such a long walk, all the farm buildings are clustered near each other. Those buildings, which were built over time at the farm, include the main house where the family lived, as well as a tourist cabin for visitors, the smokehouse, chicken coop, creamery, granary, toolshed/slaughterhouse, and the foundations of the old dairy barn. You can tour the well-interpreted farm buildings by yourself or take a guided tour of the house to learn about the family's domestic life.

The story of the property begins with the Dakin family, who settled the farm in the late 1780s, then sold it in 1793 to the Robinson family, who would keep it for nearly 200 years. The

Robinsons were among the first Americans to import Spanish merino sheep; they would prosper during the sheep craze that followed. A later generation of Robinsons would be active in the abolition movement, sheltering runaway slaves at the farm. Today the site is one of the best-documented stops along the Underground Railroad, the loose chain of stops where people were willing to care for slaves as they escaped north in the years before the Civil War.

By the twentieth century, Rokeby, like most other farms in Vermont, had converted to dairying out of economic necessity. The Robinsons also joined the tourist trade, offering overnight accommodations starting in the 1920s. Rokeby's grounds include a tourist cabin, which the Robinsons built during the 1930s to add to the capacity of their house. Then as now, people streamed into Vermont to enjoy the clean air, take in the mountain scenery, and visit working farms.

Ethan Allen Homestead & Museum

Burlington
www.ethanallenhomestead.org
802-865-4556

The museum is open from May through October. In May, from 1 to 5 p.m. daily; June through October, 10 a.m. to 5 p.m. Monday through Saturday; and from 1 p.m. to 5 p.m. Sunday. Admission to the museum, farmhouse and grounds is $15 for families, $5 for adults, $3 for children 5 to 17 years old, and free for children under 5.

Shelburne Farms

Shelburne
www.shelburnefarms.org
802-985-8686

Open from mid-May through mid-October. Admission is $6 for adults, $5 for seniors, and $4 for children ages 3 to 14. You can also pay an admission fee that includes a guided tour of the inn and a trip past the elegant Coach Barn. The 90-minute tours are offered four times daily, every two hours, starting at 9:30 a.m. Tours of the immense and ornate breeding barn are offered at 1:15 p.m. on Monday, Wednesday, Friday, and Sunday and last about 90 minutes. At 2:30 p.m. on Tuesday and Thursday, you can attend the farm's tea, and have the chance to tour the inn's main floor and gardens.

The farm's trails are open year-round.

Shelburne Museum
Shelburne
www.shelburnemuseum.org
802-985-3346

Open daily from the beginning of May through the end of October, 10 a.m. to 5 p.m. Admission is $18 for adults, $13 for students, $9 for children 6 to 18 years old, and free for children under 6.

Harrington's of Vermont
Shelburne
802-985-2000 (for the Shelburne store)
802-434-4444 (to place mail orders)

www.harringtonham.com
Harrington's retail store in Shelburne is open 7:30 a.m. to 6 p.m. weekdays and 8 a.m. to 5 p.m. weekends between Memorial Day and New Year's Eve. The store closes an hour earlier on weekdays between New Year's Day and Memorial Day.

Charlotte Berry Farm
Charlotte
802-425-3652

Open daily from late June through Halloween. Hours depend on picking conditions. You can also purchase local honey and maple syrup.

Mt. Philo State Park
Charlotte
802-425-2390
www.vtstateparks.com/htm/philo.cfm

The park is open from mid-May to October 15.

Dakin Farm
Ferrisburgh
802-425-6721
800-993-2546
www.dakinfarm.com

Open Monday through Saturday from 8 a.m. to 5 p.m. during most of the year. From

Thanksgiving through December, open seven days a week, from 8 a.m. to 6 p.m.

Rokeby Museum
Ferrisburgh
www.rokeby.org
802-877-3406

Open from mid-May through mid-October. The farm outbuildings and the farm surrounding them can be seen with a self-guided tour Tuesday through Sunday 10 a.m. to 4 p.m. Permanent exhibits are located in the outbuildings, and an audio tour is available. Forty-five-minute tours of the farmhouse are offered at 11 a.m., 12:30 p.m., and 2 p.m., Thursday through Sunday. Admission is $6 for adults, $4 for seniors and students, and $2 for children 12 and under. Rokeby's has extensive walking trails, which are open year-round during daylight hours. A self-guided tour of the woods and farmland, entitled "How a Farm Becomes a Forest," is available.

Restaurants

Penny Cluse Café
Burlington
802-660-3808
www.pennycluse.com

Penny Cluse Café serves good old American comfort food, with Southwestern spice if you want it, and plenty of vegetarian options. Entrées range from $6 to $10. Open Monday through Friday, 6:45 a.m. to 3 p.m.; weekends and Monday holidays, from 8 a.m. to 3 p.m.

Smokejack's
Burlington
802-658-1119
www.smokejacks@verizon.net

Smokejack's, which serves contemporary American cuisine, is open seven days a week. On weekdays, the restaurant serves lunch and dinner. Brunch replaces lunch on weekends. Lunch and brunch entrées range from $7 to $12. Dinner entrées cost between $12 and $21.

The Inn at Shelburne Farms
Shelburne
www.shelburnefarms.org
802-985-8498

The restaurant is open from mid-April to mid-October for breakfast, Sunday brunch, and dinner. Breakfast choices range from $6.50 to $8.75. For dinner, entrées range from $20 to $30.

Lodging

Willard Street Inn
Burlington
www.willardstreetinn.com
802-651-8710
800-577-8712

This elegant bed-and-breakfast is located in an 1880s home that sits on the hill above downtown Burlington. Room rates range from $125 to $225, and include breakfast. Rates are higher during foliage season.

The Inn at Shelburne Farms
Shelburne
www.shelburnefarms.org
802-985-8498

Open from mid-April to mid-October. Room rates vary from about $100 to nearly $400 per night.

For more lodging options, check the extensive listings at www.vermontvacation.com or call 800-VERMONT.

The Southern Champlain Valley

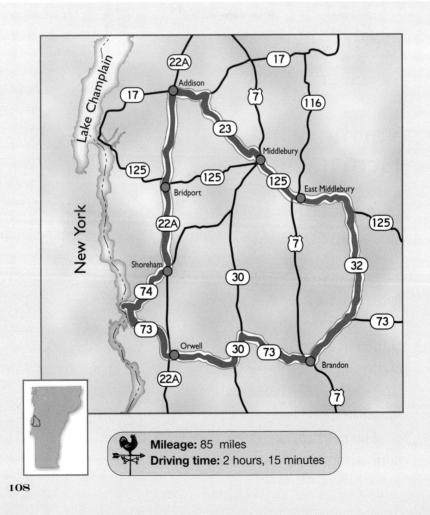

Mileage: 85 miles
Driving time: 2 hours, 15 minutes

Vermont's Agricultural Heartland

In Addison County, farming is still king—or if not king, at least part of the royal family. Here is a place where farm abuts farm for as far as the eye can see. Farmers were drawn here more than two hundred years ago for the fertile soils on relatively flat fields and the climate tempered by nearby Lake Champlain. And those factors have kept farmers in the region. While farmers in virtually every area of the state have to deal with development pressures, farmers here have been spared from the forces exerted by suburban sprawl and large-scale tourist attractions.

This tour will take you through Addison County and the northern tip of Rutland County, which contain some of

Vermont's most rich agricultural lands. Farming in this area reached its peak, at least financially, during the early 1800s, when the nation's demand for wool made local farmers rich. As you drive through the county, you'll see some grand old farmhouses built with large columns at the entrance, a style known as Greek Revival. These homes are the principal artifact you'll find today of the early nineteenth-century sheep craze, which, like the internet bubble of our own time, eventually burst.

↔ Middlebury

The tour will begin in Middlebury. The town is what it always has been, the population center and cultural hub of an otherwise agricultural area. In Vermont, however, the term "population hub" is a relative term. Middlebury has a population of roughly 8,000. Still, partly because of Middlebury College, which sits on a hill a short walk from downtown, the community has more cultural offerings than you'd expect from a town this size.

Although most Vermont towns make for pleasant places to walk, Middlebury is particularly well suited for meandering. The downtown is compact, but varied. As the county's largest town, Middlebury has a strong and diverse retail district. Also, like most Vermont communities, Middlebury has maintained its historic buildings, which add to the charm of strolling through it.

Vermont Folklife Center

People often eulogize farming culture, as if it were a thing of the past. In some cases, it is. Some traditions have died. But others live on. At the Vermont Folklife Center in Middlebury you can hear about traditions past and present from the people who have lived them. Over the years, the center has interviewed hundreds of Vermonters to capture their stories. You can get a glimpse of the work the Folklife Center does by stopping by its headquarters in Middlebury.

The center is located on Court Street, which is part of Route 7 in Middlebury, next to the Chittenden Bank. To reach it from the north, follow Route 7 into town. The road will take you past a small square on your left and then to a traffic light. The Vermont Folklife Center is straight ahead. Parking is available behind the building. If you're coming from the south, as you see the historic, four-story brick Middlebury Inn looming ahead, you will be approaching a traffic light. The Folklife Center is on the right immediately after the light.

The Vermont Folklife Center features a small museum with a rotating exhibit on various aspects of the state's past and present. The Folklife Center's work reminds us that what might seem like ancient history often continues in living memory. While visitors walk among

Sap Beer

The Vermont Folklife Center is a repository for the state's memories. Where would we be without it?

A recent exhibit included the voice of farmer Edgar Dodge, explaining the lost art of making sap beer. For those who are unfamiliar with sap beer—which probably includes pretty much everyone born after Dodge—the powerful beverage was made each spring from the last sap from the trees, mixed with sugar, corn, and whatever else folks might find. By the first cutting of hay, traditionally on July 4th, the beer was ready. Sometimes the sap beer would come out clear as good ale; other times it was "kinda stringy," Dodge explained, his thick Vermont accent pronouncing it "koynda string-ay."

Like some of the other traditions that the museum memorializes, sap beer is a thing of the past. "Doubt there's a barrel of sap beer in Vermont today," Dodge said, ". . . but I must say it was a pretty good drink for haying, a pretty good drink for haying."

the displays, they can listen on headsets to the recorded voices of Vermonters. To give you an idea of the types of stories you might hear at the center, take a recent exhibit, which included stories about life as a cook in a logging camp, about a family's tradition of Saturday night baths during the early decades of the twentieth century, or how Vermonters used to switch on a light as a signal to the man plowing the road that he was welcome to come in for a break.

Now, let's head downtown. Though it is just down the hill, the route is a bit serpentine. We are heading to Main Street, which is also Route 30/125. Drive back up the Folklife Center's driveway. Turn right onto Court Street and move immediately into the center lane. Over the next 100 yards or so, the flow of traffic will lead you left and then quickly right. Your lane will now force you to bear left, across one lane of oncoming traffic, and bring you almost immediately to a stop sign. Turn left at the sign onto Main Street. Find a parking space. We'll visit the next couple of stops on foot.

We are heading to the far side of the bridge on Main Street, which crosses the falls at Otter Creek. It was those falls that drew industry to the town two centuries ago, back when water was used to power manufacturing.

Vermont State Craft Center at Frog Hollow

After crossing the bridge at Otter Creek, take your first right onto Frog Hollow Road. This area was long a center of industry in an otherwise agricultural county. The second building on your right is the Vermont State Craft Center at Frog Hollow.

The craft school was founded in 1971 by a group of local craftspeople and community leaders as a way of providing young people an opportunity to learn from professional artists. The gallery started soon after. Since its inception the center has grown and added locations in Burlington and Manchester. Although it was started as a school, Frog Hollow is now better known for its galleries, which have become the most sought after venues for Vermont's large communities of artisans and artists. Most of the beautiful decorative and fine arts you'll find in the galleries trace their roots back to humbler beginnings. Pottery, weaving, basketry, glassblowing, wood turning—all were practical crafts made for use in everyday domestic life in agricultural communities where the people did not have the time or money to afford luxuries.

When you leave the gallery, take a moment to study the buildings along Frog Hollow Road. The Star Mill, across the street, and the large stone building down the hill from the gallery were both originally woolen mills. They were built to serve the large sheep-farming population in Addison County. In the early 1800s, Vermont, and particularly Addison County, was in the midst of the merino sheep craze. The sheep, which were originally imported from Spain, were highly prized for the excellent quality wool they produced. Since merinos were so sought after, the value of these sheep soared. A prized ram could net a fortune in stud fees. The best rams were well known in the farming community, and were worth thousands of dollars even then.

Sheldon Museum

After leaving the craft center, walk up Park Street, which is located directly across from Frog Hollow. Before you reach Main Street, you will see the Sheldon Museum on your right. This excellent small museum contains the collections of local resident Henry Sheldon, who for three decades collected and documented everyday life in Addison County.

Since Sheldon was doing his collecting in the midst of a farming area—and, indeed, grew up on a farm himself—the museum contains a fine collection of agricultural implements, such as rakes, yokes, butter churns, pitchforks, and beehives. There is even some agricultural literature.

The centerpiece of the museum may be the building in which it is housed. The Judd-Harris House is an 1829 Federal-style home where Sheldon boarded, and which he later purchased to house his museum. Decorated with nineteenth-century furniture that Sheldon collected, the rooms offer a glimpse of how some local residents used to live.

๑ Weybridge

Just south of downtown Middlebury is Weybridge, where we'll visit the home of the Morgan horse as well as a large dairy farm. As you drive from the Morgan Horse Farm to Monument Farms Dairy you'll start to get an idea of how much great agricultural land Addison County has. Here, the big hills have subsided and the land begins to flatten out. To the east of Middlebury and Weybridge are the Green Mountains, but in every other direction, the land is tamer, more suitable for farming.

Morgan Horse Farm

The Morgan Horse Farm, which features lovely pastures and ornate Victorian farm buildings, is open to the public. To reach it, drive south across the downtown bridge on Main Street. Just past the Sheldon Museum, bear right, then take your first right onto Route 23. Go .75 mile and follow the signs to the horse farm.

In addition to merino sheep, the other animal that became a symbol of Vermont agriculture was the Morgan horse. The breed traces its roots back to a single stallion, a horse named Figure, who was purchased and brought to the state in about 1790 by a Vermonter named Justin Morgan. Figure showed intelligence, strength, and an easy disposition, which made him well suited to farm work. He passed these traits on to his progeny, creating a breed that also excelled at racing and was a valued mount during the Civil War. Morgans helped settlers open the West and today are popular show and family horses.

The breed might have become extinct during the nineteenth century if not for the intervention of local philanthropist Joseph Battell. He dedicated his farm in Weybridge to the breeding of Morgans and dedicated himself to studying their pedigrees. In 1906 he donated the farm to the U.S. government, which bred, trained, exhibited, and sold Morgans there. In 1951, the government turned the farm over to the University of Vermont, which continues the work of improving the breed.

Admission to the farm grounds includes a tour of the main barn and a movie about the farm's operation.

Monument Farms Dairy
Next up we'll head out to a family dairy farm, one of only two left in the state that still processes its own milk, rather than selling it wholesale to a cooperative or other milk handler. The family began processing their own milk more than seventy-five years ago.

Monument Farms Dairy is located among a cluster of homes in an area known as Weybridge Hill. To reach the farm, return to Route 23 turn right, and follow Route 23 for 2 miles until you come to a small cluster of houses and a large monument. Turn left around the monument. (The monument is to favorite

John Deere

Back in the early 1800s Middlebury was a hard place for a young man to make his fortune, a fact for which America's farming community should be grateful. If it weren't for the intense competition in this well-established community, farmers might have had to work harder to settle the Plains.

A young man named John Deere grew up in Rutland and moved as a teenager to Middlebury to work as an apprentice at a blacksmith shop, which historians believe was located along what is now Frog Hollow Road. When Deere had trouble showing his worth in Middlebury, he moved West to where towns were just being settled and competition was less fierce. There he became famous for the iron and steel plow he invented, which proved better suited for midwestern soils than the plows settlers had brought with them from the East.

Although Deere was the inventor of a plow, the company he founded is better known today for making tractors.

son Silas Wright, who went on to become governor of New York and a vice presidential candidate.) The farm is just ahead.

Millicent James Rooney's family has farmed this particular tract of land for three generations, first moving to the area in 1784. Rooney took over doing the books from her mother forty years ago and now works with her son, two nephews, and thirty other employees.

Monument Farms is not your average dairy farm. It has succeeded by expanding, buying up nearby farmland whenever it became available. The farm now covers 1,600 acres and supports 350 cows. Monument Farms sells its milk in Addison and Chittenden Counties. By the way, the farm's thick and rich chocolate milk has had a loyal following ever since the leader of a bike touring company began touting it.

◆ West Shoreham

Now let's continue west into Addison County's apple country. Here the county's dairy farms are interspersed with orchards. To get to West Shoreham, continue heading north on Route 23 for about 4.5 miles to the junction with Route 17. Turn left onto Route 17 West and follow the road for 2.7 miles to the town of Addison, where you will turn left onto Route 22A South. From here, you will drive 13 miles south until you turn right onto Route 74 West in Shoreham. The views along the way can be spectacular, giving you a good sense of how the land lies on a broad plateau that gradually descends to Lake Champlain. Beyond the lake, you will see the peaks of the Adirondack Mountains of New York State. This section of Vermont is perfect for growing apples because of its climate, which often features warm days and cool nights.

Douglas Orchards

The first orchard we'll come to is Douglas Orchards and Cider Mill. The orchard is 1.5 miles along Route 74, on the right. Like many others, this orchard is a family business started more than a century ago. Robert and Scott Douglas are the fourth generation of their family to run the orchard. Their father, Robert, still helps out.

Although the orchard is best known for growing apples, the season starts with another fruit, strawberries, which ripen by mid-June. You can pick your own through mid-July, which is just in time for raspberry season. Apple-picking season runs from Labor Day to Thanksgiving. The Douglases grow the classic New England varieties—McIntosh, Cortland, Empire, Macoun, Northern Spy, Paula Red—and they make their own apple cider.

Another excellent orchard is located just a little farther down Route 74. Turn right out of Douglas Orchards and drive 2.2 miles until you reach Champlain Orchards on your left.

Champlain Orchards

Bill Suhr bought Champlain Orchards in 1998 and has worked with the Vermont Land Trust to conserve the property. The hill behind the orchard's buildings rises gradually to a picnic area offering panoramic views of the Green Mountains, Lake Champlain, and the Adirondacks. Suhr encourages people to stop by and have a picnic on his hill, even if they aren't in the market for apples.

Of course, visitors are also welcome to buy apples, cider, and other fruit. Beginning in July and running to October, you can pick your own organic raspberries. The first apples are available in mid-August, when the Paula Reds ripen. From then into mid-October, you can pick from the 14 varieties that Champlain Orchards grows. They include classics, such as Empire and Macoun, and less common varieties such as Honeycrisp and Red Haralson. Pumpkins are available in October and November.

⤳ Brandon

Our next stops are to the east in the town of Brandon, where we will visit a pair of farms that hearken back to the days when Vermont was

Sheep Craze

Before the cow was queen in Vermont, sheep ruled. Starting in the early eighteenth century, Vermonters developed a mania for the animals. A visitor to the state at that time would have seen the hillsides thick with sheep.

The craze is said to have started with a Vermonter named William Jarvis. While working as a diplomat in Europe during the first decade of the nineteenth century, Jarvis managed to finagle the purchase of roughly 4,000 merino sheep, which were the prized possession of the king of Spain. The animals arrived in America just as the country was trying to develop its own woolens industry. Mills popped up all over New England. By 1836, Vermont alone had 33 of them. As the number of mills multiplied, they needed more wool.

And the merino was the perfect animal to provide it. The sheep were hardy, so they were easy to care for. More important, they had fine, thick fleece.

As sheep farming grew, cows became a rarer sight in Vermont. Why put all that time and effort into producing milk, when raising sheep for wool was so much easier and more lucrative?

The number of sheep Vermont had back in those days is staggering. In 1836, roughly 285,000 Vermonters shared the state with 1.1 million sheep. By 1840, the sheep population would reach 1.7 million, or nearly six sheep for every person. No other state committed itself so strongly to sheep.

At one point, top-of-the-line breeding stock were reportedly selling for $25,000 apiece, a king's ransom in those days. The most-sought-after sheep became celebrities of sorts, and their deaths were marked in the obituary sections of newspapers.

a major wool producer. These days, you'll find that it's not just wool Vermonters are producing—they're also into alpaca fiber and goat hair.

Maple View Farm Alpacas

First up is Maple View Farm Alpacas. To reach the farm from Champlain Orchards, continue south on Route 74 for another mile, until it meets Route 73. Turn left onto Route 73 East. Over the next

6 miles the road will take you through the quaint town of Orwell, which, like Shoreham, Bridport, and Addison to the north, is part of Vermont's western apple belt. We will continue on Route 73 for another 13 miles, until we reach Brandon. As you approach the town, you will see the wooded hillsides of the Green Mountain National Forest looming to the east. When you reach Route 7, turn left, and drive about 1 mile north, where you'll see a sign for Maple View Farm. At this point, you will turn left onto Arnold District Road. Follow it for 1.1 miles, then turn left onto Adams Road, which ends at the farm. You won't be able to see the barn or the animals when you pull in, but don't worry—this is the place.

In 2000, Ed and Debbie Bratton bought the old farm set on 100 acres, restored it, and brought their first alpacas to the property. Maple View Farm is open "by chance and by appointment." The Brattons like to give visitors a hands-on experience with their soft and docile animals, which are native to South America.

Maple View Farm sells alpaca fiber in its many forms—as raw fiber, as partially processed fiber called "rovings," as fully processed fiber in the form of yarn, or in finished goods, such as scarves, mittens, sweaters, and vests. The Brattons ship their alpaca fiber to a national fiber cooperative and to a processing facility in the town of Johnson. The finished goods are made by local knitters and by the workers at the fiber co-op.

Kirby's Happy Hoofers

You don't have to own 100 acres to be a wool producer. Just ask Debbie Kirby, who raises Icelandic and Shetland sheep and Angora goats in the woods behind her ranch house located just outside the village of Brandon. She started the business in 1988. To reach her place, take Route 73 East out of town. If you're coming from Maple View Farm, follow Route 7 South into downtown Brandon, then turn left onto Route 73 and continue east. Kirby's farm is on the right, 1.5 miles after the Brandon Inn.

Kirby does not charge for visits, but she asks that you call ahead. You can also see Kirby at Brandon's farmers' market on Fridays from June through October, where she sells yarn and hand-knit mittens, hats, and socks.

✧ Ripton

From Kirby's we'll head into the Green Mountain National Forest, past Hogback Mountain and Sugar Hill, and into the town of Ripton. The town is tiny—it has a population of about 550—but it is well known among writers. It is home to Middlebury College's Bread Loaf Writers' Conference and was once home to poet Robert Frost.

To get to Ripton, continue on Route 73 East for 2.8 miles, until you see a sign directing you to Blueberry Hill Inn. Turn left. In .7 mile you will see Carlisle Hill Road on your left. Take it. This road, which will become the Goshen–Ripton Road, will take you to Ripton. Along the way, you will see meadows and mountains to your left. In 3 miles, you will pass Blueberry Hill Inn, a nice place to stay. (For more information, see the Lodging section at the end of the chapter.)

Another 5 miles down the road, having passed through the lush Moosalamoo region of the Green

Dairy and General Agricultural Stats

Vermont dairy farms are small, at least compared to farms nationally. But those little farms add up. Consider a few facts:

- As of August 2003, Vermont was home to 148,000 milk cows.

- Vermont has 617,000 acres of crop land; roughly 380,000 are managed by dairy farmers.

- The average cow in Vermont produces more than 17,000 pounds of milk each year.

- The state's dairy industry generates roughly $420 million in annual milk sales.

Mountain National Forest, with its broad vistas and intimate woods, you will reach Route 125 in Ripton. Turn right on Route 125 East and follow it for 2 miles. On your right, you will see a sign for the Robert Frost Trail. Park and take a short walk along the loop. (If you want to return to Middlebury, turn left and follow the road as it sweeps down the hill through the small village of Ripton and into East Middlebury. Follow Route 125 through town and you will meet Route 7 again. Take it north back into Middlebury.)

Robert Frost Trail

Robert Frost was New England's pastoral poet. He spent much of his life in Vermont, writing poems inspired by the state's farmlands, streams, and mountains. Here is a chance to walk through some of the woods of an area he knew well, since he taught just up the road at the Bread Loaf School of English and Writers' Conference.

This 1-mile loop through a wooded area is dotted with plaques containing some of Frost's best-known and lesser-known poems. Through his work, the poet showed the connection he felt to the region he called home.

Details

Vermont Folklife Center
Middlebury
802-388-4964
www.vermontfolklifecenter.org
　　Open Tuesday through Saturday from 11 a.m. to 4 p.m. Admission is free.

Vermont State Craft Center at Frog Hollow
Middlebury
802-388-3177
www.froghollow.org
　　Open Monday through Saturday, 10 a.m. to 5:30 p.m.; Sunday noon to 5 p.m.

Frog Hollow also has showrooms in Manchester and Burlington. Classes are offered year-round at all three sites.

Sheldon Museum
Middlebury
802-388-2117
www.henrysheldonmuseum.org

Open Tuesday through Saturday, 10 a.m. to 5 p.m. Admission is $5 for adults, $4.50 for seniors and for college students with ID, $3 for children 6 to 18. The cost for families is $12.

Morgan Horse Farm
Weybridge
802-388-2011
www.uvm.edu/morgan

Open daily for guided tours May 1 through October 31. Admission, which includes an optional tour, is $5 for adults, $4 for teenagers, and $2 for children ages 5 to 12. Tours start on the hour from 9 a.m. to 4 p.m. Special rates available for school tours and other groups by advance arrangement.

Monument Farms Dairy
Weybridge
802-545-2119

The best days to visit are Tuesday and Thursday, when the Rooneys process fluid milk between 9 and 11:30 a.m. Visitors are welcome to watch and ask questions, but it's best to call first to make sure someone will be available to show you around. You can watch the afternoon milking any weekday between 1 and 5 p.m. If you call ahead, the Rooneys may be able to arrange a weekend visit as well.

Douglas Orchards
West Shoreham
802-897-5043

Champlain Orchards
West Shoreham
802-897-2777
www.champlainorchards.com

Maple View Farm Alpacas
Brandon
802-247-5412
www.mapleviewfarmalpacas.com

It's best to call ahead to make sure someone will be there to show you around.

Kirby's Happy Hoofers
Brandon
802-247-3124

There is no charge for visits, but please call ahead.

Robert Frost Trail
Ripton
Located just off Route 125, the trail is open daily from dawn to dusk.

Restaurants

Tully and Marie's
Middlebury
802-388-4182
www.tullyandmaries.com
   Tully and Marie's serves New American Cuisine, but it is also famous locally for its pad thai and seafood. The restaurant serves lunch and dinner daily, except Sunday, when brunch is served instead of lunch. Lunch entrées range from $7 to $11, brunch items cost $5 and $8, and dinner entrées run between $9 and $25.

Café Provence
Brandon
802-247-9997
   Café Provence is a bistro serving eclectic American and French foods daily. Open for breakfast, lunch, dinner, and Sunday brunch. Larger breakfast items range from $6.50 to $7.50. Brunch entrées run from $7.25 to $9.25; lunch entrées from $8.50 to $9.50; and dinner entrées from $16 to $20.

Lodging

Blueberry Hill Inn
Goshen
802-247-6735
800-448-0707
www.blueberryhillinn.com
   This inn offers an informal atmosphere in a country setting. Rates range from $100 to $200 per person per night. The rate includes a full breakfast and a four-course dinner.

For more lodging options, check the extensive listings at www.vermontvacation.com or call 800-VERMONT.

The Hill Country

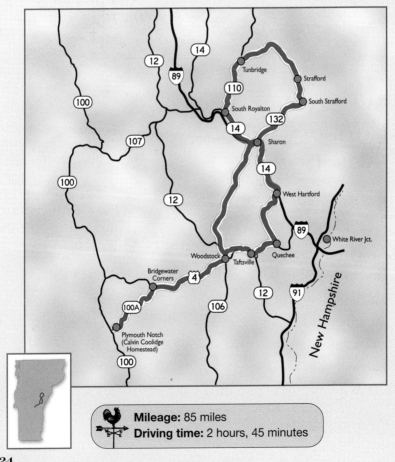

Mileage: 85 miles
Driving time: 2 hours, 45 minutes

Where Vermont's Conservation Movement Was Born

Vermont looks the way it does because of farming. Without agriculture, the state would not have its clusters of small communities surrounded by open land interspersed with woods. While farming gives Vermont much of its charm and vitality, it wasn't always that way. In the nineteenth century, overly intensive farming and logging caused soil erosion and flooding, posing a threat to the state's environment.

As a boy growing up in Woodstock in the early 1800s, George Perkins Marsh remembered noticing that the profile of nearby Mount Tom had changed after a heavy rainstorm. Marsh's experiences led him to become an early conservationist—some call him the world's first environmentalist—and to call for conscientious land stewardship. The lessons taught by Marsh, and like-minded subsequent owners of the Marsh family farm, helped change the face of farming and preserve the landscape of Vermont. The Marsh property in Woodstock is now the site of a model working farm—the Billings Farm & Museum—and the leading museum of Vermont's farming heritage.

This tour will start in Woodstock and take you through some beautiful farming country that stretches across the region's seemingly countless hills. Despite the rolling contours of the land here, this tour is contained within a large valley, the Connecticut River Valley. The river itself marks Vermont's eastern border with New Hampshire and provides the area with a longer growing season than some other sections of the state.

Along this route, you will see various forms of traditional agriculture, both on working farms and at a museum that evokes life in a farming community.

↶ Woodstock

We will start in Woodstock, a beautifully preserved and thriving village that has been a tourist destination for more than a century. The community is home to many fine restaurants and inns, as well as to a rural heritage museum and the state's only national park.

Woodstock is something of a crossroads, so it is easy to reach. The most common way to get there is by taking Route 4 West from the Woodstock exit from Interstate 89. You can also take Route 4 East from the Rutland and Killington areas. Or if you prefer quieter roads, you can reach the town by taking Route 12 South or Route 106 North.

 Side Trip

Crowley Cheese

Time traveling may be easier than it sounds. Here's one simple means to go back in time: Buy a block of Crowley cheese and eat a slice. Your taste buds will be transported back to a flavor that has been around for more than 180 years.

The Crowley Cheese Company has been in operation since 1882, which some believe makes it the oldest such company in the Western Hemisphere. And its recipe is older still, dating from 1824.

If you want more than just your sense of taste to be transported, consider taking all your senses with you on a visit to the company's factory in the hamlet of Healdville, which is about a 10-minute drive off Route 103 West from Ludlow. There you will find workers crafting cheese in the nineteenth-century factory, using nineteenth-century methods. These methods might seem outdated, but who can argue with success?

For years, people have been trying to classify Crowley's cheese. The government long ago decided it was a Colby, because it bears some resemblance. Food writers think it is more cheddar-like. But it is clearly not a Colby and it is moister and creamier than cheddar. The folks at Crowley prefer to think of it as a Crowley. Fair enough.

Factory tours are generally available on weekdays from January through October, but call ahead to make sure they will be making cheese the day of your visit. The gift shop is open year-round.

For more information, check online at www.crowleycheese-vermont.com or 800-683-2606.

Billings Farm & Museum

Billings Farm & Museum is located on Route 12, half a mile north of downtown Woodstock.

Frederick Billings might seem an unlikely champion of environmental farming and logging practices. After all, he was a Vermont lawyer who moved to California in the Gold Rush and grew fabulously wealthy from his legal practice and later by investing in railroads. While in the West, however, he saw the devastation that mining was wreaking on the land. Upon his return to Vermont, he was equally troubled by the sight of denuded hillsides, silted rivers, and failing hill farms.

Determined to show that the land could be worked with a wiser, more productive hand, he bought the Marsh family farm in Woodstock in 1871 and transformed it into a model farm and country estate. To run the operation, he hired an experienced farm manager and together they instituted a rigorous and scientific form of farm management, which was at the forefront of rural improvement at the time. He also championed the reforestation of the surrounding hills, planting 10,000 trees on former farmland in the hills above Woodstock village.

Even though Marsh and Billings never met, there was a clear link between them. Billings studied Marsh's writings, and he practiced what Marsh had preached.

Billings's farm eventually came into the possession of his granddaughter, Mary, and her husband, Laurance S. Rockefeller. Together they established the Billings Farm & Museum in 1983, with the goal of preserving and using the farm to teach about rural history and modern sustainable farming practices.

Today the Billings Farm & Museum calls itself the "Gateway to Vermont's Rural Heritage," and it truly is. The museum's exhibits and its working dairy farm offer visitors an excellent primer on farming's past. Start with the 30-minute, award-winning documentary A Place in the Land, which tells the history of this land and the three families that have worked to protect it. If you miss the start of the film, you can start with the Farm Life exhibits or explore the cow and horse barns. You can tour the museum and farm grounds quickly in an hour and a half, or take your time and spend most of the day.

The exhibits do a wonderful job of giving you the feel of what it was like to live on a farm in the nineteenth and early twentieth centuries, as well as a sense of community life back in that time. Artful

The Baaah Boom Goes Bust

Vermont farmers became rich during the sheep boom of the early 1800s. But like all booms, this one went bust.

In rushing to embrace easy profits, many Vermont farmers forgot two important economic tenets: good times don't last forever, and it pays to diversify.

The state's wool industry started unraveling in the early 1840s. Prices dropped as the federal government lowered its protective tariff on imported wool and Western farmers (including not a few transplanted Vermonters who had struggled as farmers in their home state) began raising their own sheep. With fewer profitable markets for their wool, Vermont farmers began selling their prized sheep for their meat instead of their fleece.

In recent years, Vermont farmers have regained their interest in sheep. Once again merinos and other breeds dot the state's hillsides. But this is a cautious return to sheep farming, not a return to the mania.

displays, which are housed on two floors of four connected nineteenth-century barns, show the yearly cycle of farm work along with some of the early technology that made farm life a little easier a century ago.

The museum also offers tours of its restored 1890s farmhouse, where the farm manager lived with his family and directed the work of the farm from his paneled office. In the basement is a creamery that was state of the art in its day, equipped with technology that improved the quality and healthfulness of dairy products at the turn of the nineteenth century. Today, the adjacent Dairy Bar offers locally made ice cream and other snacks that might improve your life.

Take the time to explore the barns, which house the farm's cows, horses, chickens, and sheep. If you are there at three, you can watch the afternoon milking.

If you have children, consider enrolling them in one of the educational programs Billings offers throughout the year. The varied programs are scheduled to last about three or four hours, although they can accommodate shorter or longer visits. Past programs have included "A Day in 1890: Living History for Young People," "The Draft Horse: A Partner on the Land," and "Food for Thought: Preparing the Harvest." (For more information, see the Details section at the end of this chapter.)

Across Route 12 from the museum is the mansion originally built by the Marsh family, and later the home of Frederick Billings and Mary and Laurance Rockefeller. Today it is the centerpiece of the Marsh-Billings-Rockefeller National Historical Park, which features exhibits and wooded trails focusing on forest stewardship, in addition to tours of the mansion.

Sugarbush Farm

Betsy Luce grew up on a hillside dairy farm in Woodstock. Today the farm is the center of the business she runs with her husband, Larry. Sugarbush Farm is a major attraction in the area, drawing an estimated 40,000 visitors each year, even though it's off the beaten path. Perhaps that's part of the reason. The farm perches above the valley and offers long views to the south. Despite its feeling of seclusion, the farm is not difficult to reach. The Luces have made sure to post small, helpful signs at intersections, so it is hard to get lost.

Sugarbush Farm is located about 4.5 miles from the center of town. To reach it, turn right onto River Road upon leaving the main parking lot of the Billings Farm & Museum. About a mile ahead, the road will fork. Take the left fork, which is High Pastures Road. It is aptly named. The road will climb gradually for about 2 miles, then intersect with Spaulding Lane. Turn left onto Spaulding Lane and in .2 mile turn right onto Sugarbush Farm Road. Proceed for half a mile and you will see the farm.

After you park, signs will direct you to enter what seems to be

A Farm Wife's Life

Anyone who has ever made the mistake of thinking a farm wife's life was easy should visit the Billings Farm & Museum. There, in an exhibit on everyday life in a farming community, you can read a quote from a nineteenth-century farm wife, detailing her day:

> Made a fire, mended pants, set the breakfast going, skimmed 10 pans of milk, washed the pans, ate breakfast, went to the barn and milked two cows, brought the cream out of the cellar, churned fifteen pounds of butter, made four apple pies, two mince pies, and one custard pie, done up the sink, all done at nine o'clock.

She meant 9 *a.m.*, not p.m.

the farmhouse's side door. There, you will step into a room where several workers, really friends and family, will offer you tastes of the farm's cheeses. The room doubles as the mailroom, so you'll probably see other workers packing up mail orders for shipment. Just past the cheese room you'll find another tasting room, this one for jellies, mustards, and many other types of spreads.

Look around at the cabinets and range hood, and you'll realize you are in what used to be the farmhouse kitchen. Betsy and Larry live several miles away, but rather than gut the old house and rebuild it completely, they decided to work with what they had. The decor helps remind you that, despite the place's popularity, this is still a family business.

The Luces also invite you to tour their maple sugarhouse, which features displays that provide a primer on how trees are tapped and how the sap is collected and then boiled down slowly to make syrup. You are also welcome to follow a trail the Luces have cut through their woods. The walk will take about 15 minutes. Or you can just sit at one of their picnic tables, while eating your lunch and enjoying the views of the hills rolling down the valley.

↭ Tunbridge and Strafford

Now we'll head north out of Woodstock through the lovely rolling town of Pomfret. Then we'll cross the White River at Sharon to take a bucolic drive into the archetypal hilly farming communities of Tunbridge and Strafford. To get there from Sugarbush Farm, head back down High Pasture Road and River Road, as if you were returning to Billings Farm. When you reach the museum, continue straight and turn right onto Route 12. In half a mile, the road will fork. Bear right onto Pomfret Road, leaving Route 12. Pomfret Road will then take you through a small valley split by Barnard Brook.

In 3 miles, you'll be in South Pomfret. Ahead will be Teago's General Store. Bear right just before the store and follow Pomfret Road for another 4.4 miles to a crossroads known as Hewitts Corners, where you'll turn left onto Howe Hill Road. The countryside here is mostly uplands crossed sporadically by a stream or brook. Farms appear occasionally where the land manages to level out for a stretch.

After 5 miles, the road will take you to the edge of the White River.

Man with a Plan

Tunbridge has gained local fame as the home of filmmaker John O'Brien, who has made a series of lighthearted, low-budget comedies about life in his town. O'Brien clearly admires the community's oldest generation of farmers. He has given them starring roles in his films and allowed them to ad-lib freely. The result is a loving portrait of a disappearing farming culture. Consider renting or buying a copy of one of O'Brien's movies, particularly *Man with a Plan*, to catch a glimpse of the humor and humanity of Yankee farmers in Vermont.

Turn right onto River Road and then take a left over the bridge to cross the river. Once you're on the other side, turn left onto Route 14, which snakes along beside the White River bearing you northwest. In 4 miles, you will reach the intersection with Route 110. Turn right and head north.

From here, the route will wind up through a landscape of hillocks and farms, which seem to alternate between struggling ones and others that appear more prosperous. Five miles up the valley you will find Tunbridge.

Tunbridge

When Vermonters think of farming towns, many of them think of Tunbridge. A couple of things have locked that image in Vermonters' minds. First, it has been the home of the ambitiously titled Tunbridge World's Fair. The fair started in 1867 as an agricultural fair. Over the years, it kept the farming component—complete with cattle shows and ox pulls—but added 4-H exhibits, contra dancing, carnival rides, and other attractions. For a time, the fair had an unsavory reputation for heavy drinking and girlie shows, but for years the September fair has been a popular draw for families from across the state.

As you leave the center of Tunbridge, the road will fork at a small bridge. Bear right before the bridge onto the Strafford Road (which after 3 miles is also called the Justin Morrill Memorial Highway). This route will take you through some picturesque, hilly countryside dotted with green meadows. Over the next 5 miles, the road gradually narrows until you are driving through wooded country beside the West Branch of the Ompompanoosuc River. Then the road opens out and you begin to see meadows gently rolling up the softer hills to your right. You are entering the town of Strafford.

King Arthur Flour

King Arthur Flour hasn't been around for as long as the famed knight for which it is named. It just seems that way. The company does, however, date back to the presidency of George Washington. Founded in 1790, King Arthur Flour is the oldest food company in New England. But you wouldn't know it by visiting the company's new headquarters, bakery, company store, and school in Norwich. The place is a mecca for serious bakers yet welcoming to novices.

At the store, you will find the latest in baking products, as well as the classics–everything from hard-to-find ingredients to mixes featuring King Arthur flour to Vermont food products to professional bakeware to bread machines. Just eavesdrop for a few minutes at the store and you are bound to hear a conversation between strangers drawn together by their passion for baking.

For beginners and baking professionals alike, King Arthur offers regular classes and demonstrations.

To reach King Arthur, take I-91 north to exit 13. Go straight down the off-ramp. At the light, take a left. At the next light, take another left onto Route 5 South. In less than .5 mile, you will see the company's grey building with red trim on the left.

For more information about King Arthur, or to shop online, go to www.kingarthurflour.com. The toll-free number is 800-827-6836.

Strafford Town House

As you enter the town, you'll see on your right a small hillock topped by a startlingly white clapboard building with a tall steeple. Built in 1799, originally as a church, the building has long served a different important function. It is home to Strafford's town meeting each March, at which residents act as the town's legislators and vote on the community's annual budget and other weighty matters.

Strafford residents retain some of the hardiness of the town's founders. Although the building still has no electricity or plumbing, the town's annual meeting is one of the best attended, per capita, in the state.

Take a moment to stretch your legs, walk around the building and peer in the windows. Inside, you'll see the tools of Vermont-style democracy: a stage for people to speak from, rows of seats to accommodate voters during hours of discussions, and a series of woodstoves ready to keep folks warm while they tackle the town's business.

Just down the road, you'll visit the home of another Vermonter who made a difference.

Justin Morrill Homestead

To reach the homestead, continue past the Town House into the center of town. Turn left at the stop sign and in .1 mile you'll see Morrill's house on the left.

Justin Smith Morrill is little remembered outside his native state, but he should be. He served Vermont for forty-three years in Congress during the second half of the nineteenth century. But he also served the entire country when he proposed that the federal government should create land grant colleges across the nation. The schools are named after the land that the government would grant to the states for the creation of colleges of "agriculture and the mechanical arts."

Morrill's Land Grant College Act passed in 1862. At the time, formal classical education was geared to only a few professions: lawyers, teachers, doctors, and members of the clergy. Morrill wanted to democratize education by offering practical instruction — in science, engineering, and agriculture — mixed with classical studies. The target for the curriculum was farmers and artisans, mechanics and laborers. The land grant colleges he created revolutionized farming in America by applying scientific methods to the study of agriculture for the first time.

Morrill's homestead, which is open to the public from Memorial Day to mid-October, is an excellent example of a Gothic Revival cottage, with details you might expect to see on a medieval European church. Inside, the house is decorated with original family possessions. The property includes eight agricultural outbuildings, including a horse barn, cow barn, corn barn, and ice house. The carriage barn houses an exhibit detailing Morrill's life, with special emphasis on his interest in horticulture, education, and the land grant colleges.

The state, which operates the homestead, is organizing an effort to re-create the picturesque romantic landscapes Morrill created on his home's five-acre grounds. Researchers are poring over Morrill's collection of landscaping and gardening books, which feature his own handwritten notes, to interpret his vision of Victorian perfection.

↷ Taftsville

Next we head to Taftsville, a small village within the town of Woodstock. Along the way, we will stop at a sheep farm that is open to the public. To get there, continue south on Justin Morrill Memorial Highway, through the gently undulating hills that make Strafford excellent horse country. Two miles beyond the Morrill homestead turn right onto Route 132 in South Strafford and head west. The road will continue past horse pastures. In 6 miles, you'll reach the town of Sharon. Turn left onto Route 14 and follow it roughly southeast as it parallels the White River. In another 6 miles, you'll come to a bridge over the river in West Hartford. Cross it.

You are now on the Quechee–West Hartford Road, which, as you might imagine, will take you into Quechee. There you'll find a good place to catch lunch or dinner: Simon Pearce, an elegant restaurant that serves gourmet meals, often made from local ingredients.

To continue on to Woodstock, drive as if you were returning to West Hartford on the Quechee–West Hartford Road. Half a mile out of downtown Quechee, the road will fork. Bear left onto Quechee's Main Street, which becomes River Road. In 3 miles, the road will fork. Bear left on Lower River Road down the hill and cross over the covered bridge. Exiting the bridge, bear right and drive to the stop sign. Straight ahead is Taftsville, a village within the town of Wood-

Stone Walls

Vermont wouldn't be Vermont without its stone walls. Drive along a dirt road or walk through the woods and fields and before long you'll probably bump into one.

Stone walls are as much a part of nature as anthills, according to Robert Thorson, a University of Connecticut professor who wrote about them in his book *Stone by Stone*. "The ant doesn't build these beautiful hills on purpose. The ant doesn't even care about the hills," he says. "We fixate on the ant hill, because we see it. The ant doesn't. To it, they are just disposal piles."

That is exactly what stone walls were. In the days before stone-wall building became an art form, the walls were "linear landfills," in Thorson's words. The farmers who built the walls were much more interested in clearing their fields of unwanted stones than in creating fencing.

Those walls weren't all built at once.

"I don't think people swaggered out there and just heaved the stones to the side" and constructed the wall, he says.

Some sections of Vermont had almost no stone walls at all. In the "marble belt" and slate areas of southwestern Vermont, the glaciers smashed the relatively soft rock, leaving little need to build those linear landfills.

stock. Carefully cross Route 4—the traffic can be thick and fast—
and drive to the right of the brick store/post office. Take your first
left onto Hartwood Way. When the road forks, bear left. The road
dead- ends at Shepherd's Hill Farm.

Shepherd's Hill Farm
Shepherd's Hill Farm is a recent addition to the Woodstock landscape. Ellen Terie, who opened her farm and inn in 2003, raises
sheep for meat and wool and runs an upscale bed-and-breakfast from
her home. Breakfasts feature eggs and lamb sausages from the farm's
animals. The farm, which has a wonderful view of the valley below,
is open to visitors as well as guests. Terie suggests that if you want
to come visit, you might want to call ahead to make sure someone
is home.

Taftsville Country Store
After visiting the farm, consider stopping at this wonderful country
store—it's the brick building you passed in Taftsville on your way to
Shepherd's Hill Farm. Inside the 1840 store, you'll find a great selection of local cheeses, maple syrup, and other specialty foods, as
well as a variety of fine wines.

To return to Woodstock, cross back over the covered bridge and turn
left onto River Road. The road will follow the Ottauquechee River
and soon bring you past the Billings Farm. Turning left onto Route
12 will bring you back into the center of town in half a mile.

 Side Trip

Calvin Coolidge Homestead

If you are staying in the Woodstock area more than one day, consider a trip down to President Calvin Coolidge's homestead and the village of Plymouth Notch, about a 25-minute drive from downtown Woodstock. Coolidge's farm is an interesting contrast to Billings Farm, in that the Coolidges were farmers of more modest means. To get there from Woodstock, follow Route 4 West. At Bridgewater Corners turn left onto Route 100A and follow that south to Plymouth. Follow signs to the historic site.

Calvin Coolidge is unfairly remembered as a cold and distant man of few words. He may not have talked much, but when he did, he spoke eloquently, particularly on the subject of his home state.

"I love Vermont because of her hills and valleys, her scenery and invigorating climate, but most of all because of her indomitable people," he once said. "They are a race of pioneers who have almost beggared themselves to serve others. If the spirit of liberty should vanish in other parts of the union and support of our institutions should languish, it could all be replenished from the generous store held by the people of this brave little state of Vermont."

Today, you can visit the village that won Coolidge's heart, because the place has been preserved as it would have appeared during Coolidge's childhood. Each summer and early fall, the State of Vermont, which owns and operates the site, opens 12 buildings to the public. The village cheese plant is also open.

You can tour the home where Coolidge was born and the nearby home his family moved to when he was six. It was there, while visiting as vice president in 1923, that he learned that President Harding had died and that he was now president. His father, a justice of the peace, administered Coolidge's oath of office. You can also visit the general store Coolidge's father ran, see barns featuring displays of horse-drawn vehicles and farming equipment, or walk the surrounding fields. It was in those fields that Coolidge learned the value of hard work. Even while visiting as president, he would help with the haying.

Details

Billings Farm & Museum
Woodstock
www.billingsfarm.org
802-457-2355

Open daily 10 a.m. to 5 p.m. from May 1 to October 31. Also open Thanksgiving weekend, December weekends; December 26–31; sleigh ride weekends on Martin Luther King weekend and Presidents' Day weekend. Admission: adults $9:50; seniors $8:50; children (13–17 years old) $7:50; (5–12) $5, (3–4) $3; under 3 get in for free. Educational programs cost $5 to $8 per child. For more information or to register, call weekdays between 8 a.m. and 4:30 p.m., or visit the Web site.

Sugarbush Farm
Woodstock
www.sugarbushfarm.com
802- 457-1757
800-281-1757

Open weekdays 8 a.m. to 5 p.m.; weekends and holidays, 9 a.m. to 5 p.m. (closed Thanksgiving and Christmas.) Closed some Sundays in January and February, so call ahead. In winter and early spring, call to check on road conditions; the farm is located on a dirt road.

Justin Smith Morrill Homestead
Strafford
www.historicvermont.org
802-828-3051

Open mid-May through mid-October, Wednesday through Sunday, 11 a.m. to 5 p.m. Admission is $5 for adults; children 14 and under, free. Groups of 10 or more must reserve ahead. The cost for groups is $3 per person.

Shepherd's Hill Farm
Taftsville
www.shepherdshillfarm.com
802-457-3087

Shepherd's Hill Farm is open to the public. Self-guided tours are free. Guided tours cost $3 per person.

Taftsville Country Store
Taftsville
802-457-1135

King Arthur Flour
Norwich
800-827-6836
www.kingarthurflour.com
The Baker's Store is open
Monday through Saturday, 8:30
a.m. to 6 p.m. and Sunday from
8:30 a.m. to 4 p.m. Check Web
site for details on upcoming
demonstrations and classes.

Calvin Coolidge Homestead
Plymouth Notch
802-672-3773 for information
weekdays from 9 a.m. to 5 p.m.
www.historicvermont.org
    Open daily Memorial Day
through mid-October. Admission
is $7.50 for adults, $2 for
children 6–14, and free for
children under 6.

Restaurants

Simon Pearce
Quechee
802-295-1470
www.simonpearce.com/
CSTM_restaurants.aspx
    The restaurant, which serves
both lunch and dinner, offers
what it terms "creative American
cuisine." Lunch entrées range

from $9 to $13. Dinner choices
range from $20 to $32.
Reservations are appreciated.

The Woodstock area also boasts
many other fine restaurants that
serve meals prepared with local
ingredients.

Lodging

Shepherd's Hill Farm
Taftsville
802-457-3087
www.shepherdshillfarm.com
    The bed-and-breakfast offers
two bedrooms with shared bath
and a family suite. The cost per
night is $135 to $150 for the
single bedrooms and $325 for the
suite. Rates may be higher
during peak season. Ask about
specials when you call.

For more lodging options, check
the extensive listings at
www.vermontvacation.com or
call 800-VERMONT.

TOUR 8

Southwestern Vermont

Mileage: 35 miles
Driving time: 1 hour

Diversity in a Small Valley

This tour will take you through the Valley of Vermont. A narrow slit of land bordered on the east by the Green Mountains and on the west by the Taconics, the valley runs from the Massachusetts border north to just south of the town of Brandon. At first glance, the area might seem inhospitable to farming—the valley is no more than eight miles wide and the surrounding peaks tend to block out early and late light. Less obvious, however, is the limestone rock that cradles the valley and contributes to its particularly rich soil. Farms squeeze between the mountains and the creeks and rivers that run through the valley. Sometimes the agricultural land even mounts the flanks of those high hills.

To get a good sense of the Valley of Vermont, head south out of Bennington on Route 7. A little more than a mile out of the center of town, you will pass the Apple Barn & Country Bakeshop on your left. We'll come back to it in a moment. Less than half a mile south of the Apple Barn, you will see Carpenter Hill Road on your right. Turn right and go straight up the hill; don't take the fork onto Monument Avenue.

Follow Carpenter Hill Road about 2 miles to where the pavement ends. The whole time you'll be driving through **Southern Vermont Orchards**, which was once the largest privately owned orchard in the world, stretching for 10 miles. The orchards were created by Edward Hamlin Everett starting in 1912. In addition to growing 65 varieties of apples, the orchard also produced cherries, plums, pears, and quince. Southern Vermont Orchards covers 300 acres today and is owned by the same family that owns the Apple Barn.

Now that you are high on Carpenter Hill, take a look around. To the north you will have a spectacular view of the valley, which runs nearly half the length of Vermont. We will explore there now, visiting a wide range of farming operations, and making a couple of side trips related to artists who were inspired by the spirit of Vermont. This tour will take us from Bennington through Shaftsbury and Arlington and end at Manchester. Among our stops will be a major apple grower that has evolved to offer much more; an alpaca farmer, part of a new breed of agriculturalists popping up in the state; an excellent small farm-based ice cream maker you've probably never heard of; a nursery that is a hub in its community; and the estate of a Lincoln that is teaching the value of alternative agriculture.

↬ Bennington

When Europeans first settled in Vermont, Bennington was one of the places they chose. They came for the fertile soil and relatively mild climate, and also probably because the area was so close to the border of Massachusetts, where the land had already been pretty much divvied up. The area around Bennington was part of the first land grant issued by the governor of New Hampshire, which at the time claimed the area that is today known as Vermont. So in 1750, when Gov. Benning Wentworth issued the grant, the town earned the honor of being named after him.

Since that day, Bennington has always been one of Vermont's best-known communities. First we will visit one of the best-known businesses in that community.

The Apple Barn

As you head back north on Route 7, pull in at the Apple Barn, which will be on your right. The building offers an amazing variety of Vermont-made foods, many of them produced by the people at the Apple Barn. You'll find maple syrup and candies, cheeses, honeys, jellies, butters, steak sauce, salad dressing, mustards, pickled beans, beets, asparagus—you name it. Even wines. And, of course, all kinds of apples.

Many of those apples end up in the bake shop's pies. The Apple Barn makes apple pie, apple-cherry pie, apple-raisin, apple-peach, apple-blackberry, and apple-cranberry, among others. Not to mention blueberry pie, peach pie, cherry pie, and so on.

Harry Diamond, whose family has owned the Apple Barn for more than thirty years, is always adding a new product or a fun activity to the mix. Outside, you'll find a corn maze and a giant slingshot, with which you can shoot apples across a large field at a target. Diamond seems particularly proud of Lilly, the Apple Barn's pumpkin-eating dinosaur. He says that other places might have pumpkin-eating dinosaurs (they do?!), but Lilly is the world's only mobile one.

By the way, if the Apple Barn sounds familiar, it might be because it has been featured recently on a number of national cooking and travel shows.

Next we'll head north of Bennington on Route 67A. From the Apple Barn, take Route 7 north through downtown Bennington. A little more than 1 mile from the center of town, turn left onto Route 7A. Follow 7A for a little less than a mile, where you will meet Route 67A. Follow 67A to North Bennington. While in North Bennington, consider a stop at Powers Market.

Powers Market

You can't miss it—it's the large Greek Revival building, with the massive columns that you'll see on your right. The building was constructed in 1835 as a company store for a nearby factory. At one time it housed the town's post office, Masonic Lodge, and library. Today it is a market, where you can pick up deli sandwiches, artfully made salads, a bottle of wine, or coffee from a Brattleboro hangout, Mocha Joe's.

While in North Bennington, you'll see signs for the Park-McCullough House, an outstanding example of Victorian architecture. If architecture interests you, this house is worth a visit.

↝ Shaftsbury

Vermont conjures many images in people's minds—white steeples, black and white cows, green mountains, red leaves—but when it conjures words, they are often those of poet Robert Frost. Though he was born in California, Frost spent a good portion of his working life writing and teaching among the fields, villages, and mountains of Vermont. Frost wrote some of his most famous poems while living in the town of Shaftsbury.

Shaftsbury Alpacas

Shaftsbury is also home to some transplanted New Yorkers who are raising alpacas. Their farm is our next stop. To find Shaftsbury Alpacas, pick up Route 67 West in North Bennington. The farm is located on the right, 2 miles out of the center of North Bennington, just before the New York State line.

Johan and Sandy Harder have joined the growing number of Vermont farmers who are raising exotic animals in the Green Mountain State. These days it is not unusual to see alpacas, llamas, or even emus (Australian birds related to the ostrich) grazing in a field here. The animals fill a niche for farmers trying to diversify to make ends meet, as well as for small-scale and hobby farmers.

The Harders and their alpacas are new to Vermont. In fact, they are here almost by accident. The Harders were living in New York City,

but knew they wanted to become alpaca farmers. While researching the business in upstate New York, they took a wrong turn and saw a sign welcoming them to Vermont. Just past the sign, they saw a property with a small barn, and a FOR SALE sign. Looking around the valley it was situated in and the mountains rising above, they fell in love with the place. And that's how the Harders arrived in Shaftsbury in 2002 and launched their business.

They may be new to the field, but they are eager to share their knowledge with others who are con-

An Alternative to Wool

Alpacas, which are native to South America, are known for their easy disposition and soft coats. Alpaca owners rave that the animal's fiber–don't call it "wool"–is an excellent alternative to lamb's wool. It contains no lanolin and is softer than wool, so it can be worn by people who are allergic to wool or find it too scratchy.

sidering raising alpacas, or with people who just like animals and want to know more about them. The Harders sell some finished alpaca fiber goods—hats, sweaters, vests, scarves, mittens, and more—from the Alpaca Shack store, which is located on their property.

Robert Frost Stone House Museum

The house Robert Frost called home during the 1920s is located on Route 7A and was recently turned into a museum. To reach it, return to the center of North Bennington and pick up Route 67 East (toward Shaftsbury), following it to the junction with Route 7A. Turn right and follow Route 7A for 1.1 miles south. The museum will be on your right.

The Robert Frost Stone House Museum, founded by a nonprofit literary group named the Friends of Robert Frost, opened in 2002. The museum contains educational exhibits on Frost's life and art.

The museum's grounds contain features that played a role in the poet's work: stone walls, birches, apple trees, meadows, and fields. Allow about an hour to tour the museum and grounds. (Frost devotees may also want to visit his grave behind the Old First Congregational Church in Bennington. The church is located on Route 9, west of the center of town.)

↬ Arlington

Next we'll head north along Route 7A, through the village of Shaftsbury and into another town that inspired Vermont artists, Arlington. Both author Dorothy Canfield Fisher and artist Norman Rockwell lived in Arlington for much of their professional careers. Fisher grew up in Kansas, but settled in Arlington on land her family had long owned. Writing from her home base in Arlington, Fisher became one of the most famous authors of her generation. Works like her *Hillsboro People* short stories and *Seasoned Timber* show the influence the state had on her.

Norman Rockwell Exhibition and Gift Shop

Rockwell lived and painted in Arlington for fourteen years, from 1939 to 1953. As many as two hundred residents of the town served as models for his depictions of small-town life. While here, Rockwell and his wife socialized with the Fishers and other artists in the area. They also participated in the public life of the town, joining local organizations and attending school and town meetings. The Norman

Rockwell Exhibition, located in a converted church in the center of the village (on Route 7A), contains reproductions of some of his works, as well as memorabilia from his time here.

The artist's former home is located off Route 313 in Arlington and is now open as the Inn at Covered Bridge Green. (See Lodging listing at the end of the chapter.)

↝ Manchester

As you continue north on Route 7A, you will notice the valley gradually narrowing. The Valley of Vermont is a cozy spot, with the Taconic Mountains to the west and the Green Mountains to the east. The distance between the ranges is perhaps a mile in some stretches here. Still, farmers have managed to find plenty of fertile land to operate.

Wilcox's Dairy

One of those farms belongs to the Wilcox family, who have been milking cows and making ice cream since 1928. You'll find their farm on the left, 5 miles north of Arlington. The operation is now run by brothers Howard and Gerald Wilcox and their families. Gerald is in charge of producing the milk (the Wilcoxes milk about 80 cows), and Howard runs the ice cream–making operation.

The business survived a devastating fire in 2001, which destroyed the barn and ice cream–making facility. The family found other places to keep the cows and make the ice cream while they rebuilt.

Wilcox's Ice Cream is sold within a 100-mile radius of the farm, but you can also get it right there at the farm's small stand. Chairs and tables are arranged in the nearby garden in case you want to enjoy your cone there. The Wilcoxes make about 30 flavors; you can find 16 of them for sale at the stand. They offer classic flavors and some less common ones, such as Sweet Cream Ginger, White

Mountain Raspberry (vanilla ice cream with white chocolate and raspberries), and Maple, which is the most popular.

Equinox Valley Nursery

Just half a mile up the road from Wilcox's, on the right side of the road, you'll find the Equinox Valley Nursery, which is a popular spot among both locals and visitors. Penny and Roger Preuss, who have been running the nursery for nearly thirty years, were drawn to the spot by the area's natural beauty; here, the Taconics and the Green Mountains are so close, they seem to embrace the nursery and the surrounding land.

Over the years the nursery has grown into a major garden center for the area. Its 17 greenhouses hold 1,200 varieties of perennials (including the classic varieties and the most newly developed ones), as well as a broad range of annuals (including some you'll have a hard time finding elsewhere) and vegetables. Equinox Valley Nursery also has a large collection of dwarf, roughly bonsai-sized, conifers for sale.

The Preusses designed the nursery as a place to linger. Grab a cup of cider and a donut and walk through the display gardens or have a seat on their new terrace. In winter and spring, the tropical conservatory is open for visitors to sit among the greenness, read the paper, and drink a cup of coffee.

In the fall, the nursery also offers a corn maze, a pumpkin patch populated by whimsically painted pumpkin-headed scarecrows, and wagon rides through what is literally the back forty (where in the past visitors have seen wild turkeys, deer, and even a bald eagle).

Hildene

Just up the road on Route 7A is perhaps the grandest house in a town full of them. Robert Todd Lincoln, son of the president, built a summer house, a mansion really, situated on 400 acres of fields and woods, and named it Hildene, meaning "hill and valley." After the death of its owner, Robert's granddaughter, a local nonprofit group purchased the place in 1975.

The house contains many furnishings and mementos of the

president and draws many Civil War buffs. Similarly, the formal gardens attract gardening enthusiasts. Visitors are also invited to wander through the surrounding fields.

The directors of Hildene are trying to add a new focus: small-scale, environmentally sensitive agriculture. They call it "niche agriculture," the kind you can do if you have at least three or four acres you can fence in. The goal is to teach people about agricultural projects they can take on at home, without having farming take over their lives. Hildene now raises beefalo, pigs, alpacas, chickens, lambs, and goats, but all on a small scale.

Hildene aims to be a showcase for modern techniques that can make small-scale farming more feasible. By setting an example of what is possible through innovation, Hildene hopes to add a few new members to the diverse mix of farmers who rely on the fertility of the Valley of Vermont.

Rent-a-Chicken

Hildene offers a special hands-on learning experience for those who don't mind having a chicken on their hands. The rent-a-chicken program is designed to teach children about raising farm animals. Children, generally ages 5 to 10, are given two chickens, a cage, and a month's worth of feed for the birds. During that month, the children record the chickens' feedings and how many eggs they produce. At the month's end, they return the chickens, and the organization then trains the next set of children who will take care of the birds.

Details

The Apple Barn & Country Bakeshop
Bennington
802-447-7780
www.theapplebarn.com
    The Apple Barn is open daily from 8:30 a.m. to 5 p.m.

Powers Market
North Bennington
802-442-6821

Shaftsbury Alpacas
Shaftsbury
802-447-3992

www.shaftsburyalpacas.com

Open most weekdays from 10 a.m. to 4 p.m. and weekends from 11 a.m. to 3 p.m., but it is best to call ahead.

Robert Frost Stone House Museum

Shaftsbury
802-447-6200
www.frostfriends.org/
stonehouse.html

Open Tuesday through Sunday 10 a.m. to 5 p.m., from May 1 to December 30. Admission is $5 for adults; $2.50 for students under 18; children under 6 get in free.

Norman Rockwell Exhibition and Gift Shop

Arlington
802-375-6423
www.vmga.org/bennington/
normrockwell.html

The museum features hundreds of reproductions of Rockwell's works. Open daily, May 1 to October 31 from 9 a.m. to 5 p.m.; November 1 to April 30 10 a.m. to 4 p.m. Between 11 a.m. and 4 p.m., one of the local residents who posed for Rockwell is available to answer questions. Admission is $1; children 12 and under get in free.

Wilcox's Dairy

Manchester
802-362-1223
www.wilcoxicecream.com

The scoop shop is open from noon to 6 p.m., Memorial Day through October.

Equinox Valley Nursery

Manchester
802-362-2610
www.equinoxvalleynursery.com

Open Monday through Saturday, 8 a.m. to 5 p.m.; Sunday 9 a.m. to 4 p.m. From January through April 1, the hours are 9 a.m. to 4 p.m. daily.

Hildene

Manchester
802-362-1788
www.hildene.org

Tours of the house and gardens are available from May 10 to October 31. Tour passes, which include passes to the grounds, cost $10 for adults (15 and older); $4 for children ages 6 to 14; children age 5 and younger get in free.

Passes to the grounds are $5 for adults (15 and older) and $2 for children ages 6 to 14; children age 5 and younger get in free. In the winter, the walking trails become ski and snowshoeing trails. Passes range from $6 to $10, depending on age and day of the week. Ski and snowshoe rentals are available.

Restaurants

The Perfect Wife Restaurant and Tavern

Manchester

802-362-2817

Chef/owner Amy Chamberlain offers an eclectic menu using many locally produced ingredients. Open Monday through Saturday, closed most Sundays. At the restaurant, which is open 5 to 10 p.m., entrées are $14 to $28; the tavern entrées range from $8 to $17. The tavern is open from 4 p.m. to closing. Reservations are recommended for the restaurant.

The Arlington Inn

Arlington

800-443-9442

Open from 5:30 to 9 p.m. Tuesday through Sunday from mid-June through October. The rest of the year, it is open the same hours, Tuesday through Saturday. The restaurant serves regional New England, American, and Continental cuisine. Entrées range from $24 to $32.

Lodging

Inn at Covered Bridge Green

Arlington

www.coveredbridgegreen.com

802-375-9489

800-726-9480

The home of painter Norman Rockwell during his years in Arlington is now a 10-room inn located west of the village. Rates, based on double occupancy, are $130 to $225, depending on season, room size, and amenities.

West Mountain Inn

Arlington

802-375-6553

www.westmountaininn.com

The inn is located in a century-old, seven-gabled home that sits among woods and field. The area features hiking and ski trails and other outdoor diversions. Room rates, which include a full country breakfast, range from $169 to $305, depending on the season.

For more lodging options, check the extensive listings at www.vermontvacation.com or call 800-VERMONT.

Southeastern Vermont

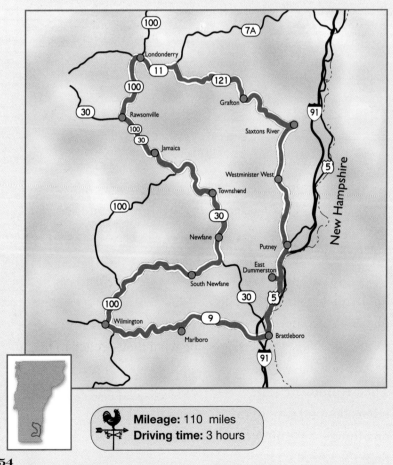

Mileage: 110 miles
Driving time: 3 hours

An Enduring Commitment

When Europeans first settled Vermont in the mid-1700s, many chose the strip of land along the Connecticut River just north and south of Brattleboro, attracted by its rich soil and its climate, which is milder than that of much of the state.

Today, residents of southeastern Vermont—some of them related to early settlers, others more recent transplants—still appreciate those qualities. Whereas settlers were subsistence farmers, growing what they needed to live, people now have a choice, and many have chosen to farm. Their reasons are varied: some do it out of family tradition; others do it for love of the land. But they have in common one thing—a commitment to keeping agriculture a part of their community's culture.

This tour will take us on a loop starting in Brattleboro and heading through Wilmington, South Newfane, Townshend, Londonderry, Grafton, Westminster, and Dummerston. Along the way, we will meet longtime dairy farmers who have diversified to stay profitable, apple growers who are working orchards established generations ago, and a new type of agriculturalist on the Vermont landscape: cheesemakers who make small batches of artisanal cheeses that are drawing international attention.

◆ Brattleboro

Brattleboro has seen a lot of action for a small community (population 12,000). It was granted in 1753, just three years after Bennington to the west (a grant was a territorial division granted by the colonial government). It was long an important train hub, the home of a major manufacturer of organs, and a magnet for artists. The town counts among its former residents author Rudyard Kipling, who wrote his *Jungle Book* just north of here in Dummerston.

Brattleboro also has a long legacy as good farming country. Farmers, whose fields sit near the Connecticut River and gradually rise up the hills to the west, have been drawn here by the area's relatively long growing season. We will start our tour with a dairy farm located in the western part of town.

Robb Family Farm

To reach the Robb Family Farm, take Interstate 91 to Exit 2. Then get on to Route 9 West. (You can also pick up Route 9 West from downtown Brattleboro.) Follow Route 9 for 1.8 miles. Turn left onto Green Leaf Street just past the 7-Eleven store. The farm is located about 3 miles from Route 9. Stay on Green Leaf for 1.5 miles. At the fork, go straight onto Ames Hill Road (a dirt road). The farm is 1.5 miles ahead on the right. The store (see page 158) is on the left.

Charles and Helen Robb's classic white farmhouse sits beside the road. Rolling green meadows fill clearings in the woods. The place must look much as it did a century ago when members of the Robb family moved their dairy farm here. Still, this is not a time capsule. Things have changed. The Robbs recently added a new milking parlor and a free-stall barn to make milking and feeding easier and the cows more comfortable.

Across the dirt road from the farmhouse is something else that's new. Connected to the family's maple sugaring house, the Robbs

Strolling of the Heifers

Vermonters love their rural heritage. If you happened to be in Brattleboro during the first weekend in June, you'll learn just how much. That's when the town and surrounding communities celebrate the Strolling of the Heifers. The four-day event, which has drawn more than 30,000 visitors, gets its name from a bovine parade down Main Street featuring dozens of flower-bedecked calves and heifers being led by 4-H Club members, local school students, and area farmers. The parade is a lighthearted tribute to farming. Some of the participants wear goofy cow costumes and tote signs with outrageous puns like "Moochas Gracias" and "I'm having an udderly good time."

The festival, however, has a serious purpose: to teach people the importance of agriculture in their daily lives and to encourage local children to become involved in farming. In addition to the parade, organizers fill the weekend with farm-related activities. They offer tours of area farms, discussions of issues facing farmers, a square dance, a celebrity milking contest, hay rides, a Heifer Ball at which chefs create gourmet menus relying almost entirely on locally produced ingredients, and an art show featuring works that depict agriculture.

For more information, check online at www.strollingoftheheifers.com or call 877-887-2370.

have added a store. Helen Robb runs the Country Shop while Charles and their son, Charles Jr., do the milking and sugaring. From the store, Helen sells the farm's maple syrup, maple candy, maple cream, and maple drizzle, for putting on ice cream. She also sells the works of a local potter, Vermont cheeses, and many other Vermont products.

The store helps the Robbs supplement the income they get from milking 60 cows and boiling down the sap from 1,800 tree taps. Much of what they sell is through mail order, so Helen has to "borrow" her husband for a couple weeks as the holidays approach each year to get the shipping done.

If you call ahead, the Robbs also offer wagon and sleigh rides through some of the farm's 360 acres.

↩ Wilmington

Now we'll embark on a scenic drive from Brattleboro to Wilmington. To reach Wilmington from the Robb Family Farm, continue west on Ames Hill Road for about 4 miles, and you'll come to the center of the tiny village of Marlboro. Turn right onto the pavement and then almost immediately bear left onto Town Hill Road, a dirt road. In about a mile the road will end at Route 9. Turn left and follow Route 9 West.

The road gradually begins to climb, and after about 3 miles you are cresting the ridge on Hogback Mountain. The area has pull-offs where you can admire the 100-mile view south into Massachusetts and east into New Hampshire. From here, the road descends the west side of the mountain, and in 5 miles you'll reach downtown Wilmington.

Adams Farm

Since the end of the Civil War, Adamses have lived on this farm in Wilmington. During the nearly 150 years that the family has owned the property, seemingly every generation has had to adapt to a changing economy and come up with new ways to make the farm thrive. In that way, the Adamses are a great example of how agriculture has evolved in this state.

To reach the farm, from downtown Wilmington get onto Route 100 North and follow it for 3 miles, until you reach Higley Hill Road on your right. Turn here and you will see Adams Farm just ahead on the right.

Henry and Sarah Adams bought the property in 1865 and started the farm. By the 1880s they were among the first wave of Vermont farmers to welcome guests into their homes when they opened a bed-and-breakfast. In the 1930s, a later generation augmented the farm's dairying income by more heavily logging the property. They also kept running the bed-and-breakfast and were now running it through the winter to cater to people who had taken up the nascent sport of alpine skiing.

In 1969, a new generation of Adamses chose to go more seriously into dairying, increasing the size of the herd and closing the bed-and-breakfast. Then, in 1986, with the nation experiencing a milk glut that drove down prices, the Adamses sold their cows as part of a federal buyout program, but continued to make syrup, offer sleigh rides, and raise crops.

Since 1993, when the newest generation took over the farm, Jill Adams Mancivalano and her husband, Carl, have again made farm visits a centerpiece of the business, while maintaining the place as a working farm. Today, the Mancivalanos seem to live by the credo that variety is the spice of life. Start with the types of animals they raise: draft horses, miniature donkeys, ducks, chickens, sheep, goats, rabbits, pigs, llamas. And that's just a partial list.

Visiting the farm in summer or fall, you might pet the animals, bottle-feed a calf or lamb, gather eggs, or learn how to milk a goat. Or you might watch a sheepherding demonstration, take a wagon ride out to an evening bonfire, or browse the farm store, which is stocked with goods made on the property and elsewhere in

Vermont. In winter, a sleigh replaces the wagon, the animals are in the barn, and the hours are shorter, but the Mancivalanos keep the schedule packed with such activities as snowshoeing and holiday-related events.

↝ Newfane

Next, we'll head to a well-known nursery and orchard that draws people from far away to the village of South Newfane, and then we'll go to a farm stand in Newfane that epitomizes the bounty of the land.

Olallie Daylily Gardens

The gardens are located just south of the Newfane village center. To get there, return to Route 100 in Wilmington and continue north, taking your first right onto East Dover Road near the Sitzmark Golf Course. In a mile, the road will seem to dead-end at a T intersection. Turn right and continue following it for the next 8 miles through East Dover and into South Newfane. Along this stretch, you will be greeted with some sensational views of the hills to the north and east before you wind into town. The road will reach a stop sign in South Newfane. Turn right onto Auger Hole Road. Olallie Daylily Gardens is 1 mile down on your left.

Christopher and Amelia Darrow at Olallie Daylily Gardens grow more than 1,000 varieties of daylilies and 60 varieties of Siberian iris, as well as 400 high-bush blueberries you can pick yourself in July and August.

The business literally grew out of a family passion. Starting in the 1950s, Christopher's grandfather, Dr. George Darrow, became an avid collector and hybridizer of daylilies. In 1979, Darrow decided to pass on what he had created, so he invited Christopher and his parents to visit his Olallie Farm in Maryland and dig up some of his daylilies. The plants became the starting point for Olallie Daylily Gardens, which Christopher and his wife, Amelia, opened in Vermont in 1980.

If you will be passing through town outside of regular business hours, you can call to set up an appointment.

Dutton Farm Stand
From Olallie Daylily Gardens, return to the center of South Newfane and continue straight, following the main road (Dover Road)

Gigantic Roadside Marshmallows

As you've been driving around Vermont, you may have been wondering what all those giant marshmallows in the fields are. If you are not from a farming area, your confusion is understandable. Those odd-looking, blindingly white masses are a fairly recent arrival here. They are merely round hay bales wrapped in plastic. Their cousins are those things that look like immense white caterpillars, which are actually covered haylage or silage.

A couple of definitions might be in order here. Haylage is like hay in that it is chopped grass, but it is moister. Silage in Vermont is typically chopped corn, although it can contain other grains. Whatever is under those plastic wraps—hay, haylage, or silage—is used for animal feed.

Another way to store feed that you'll see is a so-called bunker silo, which is like a large concrete box with no top. In lieu of a top, farmers cover the feed with white plastic weighted down with old tires.

All these storage devices—the marshmallows, caterpillars, and bunker silos—do the same job as traditional silos: keep out oxygen that can lead to rot—and they are a low-cost solution to storing feed. They may not be as picturesque as conventional silos, but if they can keep more farms in business and more land in production, they have a certain allure.

through town. This will lead you through a narrow valley and in little more than a mile across a one-lane covered bridge. You are about to enter the quaint village of Williamsville, where the road you're on will become Grimes Hill Road. Follow it for 1.6 miles until it ends at Route 30. Turn left to follow Route 30 North. Dutton Farm Stand is just ahead on your left.

For more than twenty years, Wendy and Paul Dutton's business has been growing, in more ways than one. The couple has created a wide-ranging agricultural enterprise that involves growing a multitude of crops in a number of locations, and selling them at several stores across southern Vermont. We are about to pass one of those stores in Newfane.

The farm stand sells an amazing array of foods grown on 150 acres located in several towns. The Duttons grow crops—such as blueberries, strawberries, raspberries, and apples—on land in Brattleboro, Windham, Newfane, and Brookline. They make maple sugar on their property in Manchester. Dutton Farm Stands also offer vegetables that run the gamut from asparagus to zucchini, as well as apples, their own cider, berries, pies, soft-serve ice cream, and much more. Perhaps most amazing is that the Duttons grow or make 75 percent of what they sell.

To sell all these farm products, the Duttons operate two other farm stands, one on Route 30/11 in Manchester; the other on Route 9 in West Brattleboro.

Vermont has long been known for its excellent cheddar cheeses. Now a new breed of cheesemakers has entered the scene, adding richness and diversity to the state's reputation. Many of those cheesemakers call this part of Vermont home. At our next three stops— Townshend, Londonderry, and Grafton—we'll visit a couple of those cheesemakers, along with a renowned producer of cheddar, before we head south into the region's apple-growing belt.

↝ Townshend

The first stop on this cheese tour is Peaked Mountain Farm in Townshend. The landscape here is rugged, the hills rough-edged and rocky. To reach Townshend, continue north on Route 30 after leaving the Dutton Farm Stand. You will soon pass through the village of Newfane. Continue for 4.5 miles, and you will reach the center of Townshend, where you will bear right onto Route 35. Quickly take your first right onto Peaked Mountain Road. The road will turn to dirt and cut along a hillside. Stone walls line the road as it leads upward. In 1.5 miles you will reach Peaked Mountain Farm.

Peaked Mountain Farm

Bob and Ann Works left the high-stress world of the New York City area a decade ago to take on jobs that were equally demanding, but which they could do with their hands. They purchased a historic 100-acre farm that was formerly home to dairy cows and horses. Today, sheep roam the pastures of their Peaked Mountain Farm.

The Workses use the sheep's milk to produce the farm's sought after varieties of farmstead cheeses. They make the cheese by hand, rather than relying on machinery, and they age it on the property. The cheeses are all unpasteurized. The aging process ensures the cheese's safety and heightens its flavor.

Among Peaked Farms' cheeses are Ewe-Jersey, Vermont Dandy, and Camembert Bo-Peep. Each year the Workses also produce a few experimental cheeses to consider for inclusion in their product line the following year. The Workses sell their cheeses at area food markets, as well as in Massachusetts, Connecticut, and the New York City area. They sell their own lamb, sausages, pâtés, maple syrup, breads, and cookies at a small farmstead shop and at local farmers' markets.

Visitors are welcome any day, because someone is always home working—it's a farm after all. Be advised, however, that since this is a working farm, the Workses will spare what time they have from their busy schedules.

☙ Londonderry

To reach the next cheesemaker on this tour, return down Peaked Mountain Road to the center of Townshend and turn right on Route 30 North. We are heading 20 miles up the road to Londonderry to the Taylor Farm. Route 30 will wind along the West River, past the Townshend Dam, and through the tiny villages of West Townshend and East Jamaica. Next, you'll pass through Jamaica, a small town that despite its name is known for its connection with cold-weather tourism, because of its proximity to Stratton Mountain. Routes 30 and 100 are sharing the road for a stretch, but about 4.5 miles north of Jamaica you will reach the small village of Rawsonville, where you will veer right and continue on Route 100 North. Londonderry is another 6 miles ahead.

When you reach Londonderry, turn left onto Route 11 West. After 1 mile you'll see the Taylor Farm on your right.

Taylor Farm

Like the Workses, Jon and Jill Wright arrived in Vermont from the New York City area. Jon had an attraction to the area, having spent summers here. As a seventeen-year-old, he even worked on the Taylor Farm. Then, in his thirties, he returned and bought it.

The Wrights knew they wanted to become cheesemakers, and Jill tried numerous recipes before deciding to make the European-style raw milk Farmhouse Gouda that you can now find at fine food stores around the state. Under the Taylor Farm name, the Wrights now produce numerous other versions of Gouda, including Maple Smoke Gouda and Aged Gouda, as well as others flavored with garlic, chipotle, cumin, caraway, or nettles.

You can, of course, buy Taylor Farm cheeses at the farm. If you would like to take a tour of the cheesemaking room or the farm, someone is usually available to show you around. And if you would like to be there for the afternoon milking, show up around 4 p.m.

The Wrights try to live lightly on the land and treat their animals well. They graze their Holsteins on pastures that are naturally fertilized. Their cows are individually named and never treated with growth hormones. In addition, the Wrights recently sold their development rights to the Vermont Land Trust, preserving the farm for future generations.

⟿ Grafton

While the Wrights and the Workses are helping give Vermont a new reputation for fine artisanal cheeses, the state still has some excellent cheddar makers. One is down the road in Grafton. The town was once a bustling, prosperous community, which had grown rich on soapstone quarrying and sheep farming. But it started to fall on hard times in the 1840s. During some of its down years, however, it could boast a cheese factory—the Grafton Cooperative Cheese Factory—which was founded in 1892. The factory lasted only 20 years before it was lost in a fire.

Half a century later, when a philanthropist with local ties founded the Windham Foundation to restore the town to its former glory, Grafton's cheese factory was reborn. Today Grafton is the sort of village that people picture when they think of Vermont. Its many historic white clapboard buildings, which include the famous Grafton Inn and stores, are exquisitely preserved and cluster around a village green. The community also has other features that give it an untouched air, including a working blacksmith shop, a sheep farm, and the aptly named Old Tavern, a restaurant and inn that dates back to 1801.

To reach Grafton from the Taylor Farm, turn left out of the driveway onto Route 11, heading east. Follow Route 11 for almost 6 miles into North Windham, where you will turn right onto Route 121 East headed toward Grafton. For nearly 10 miles, the road tries to follow every bend and twist of Saxtons River as it flows to Grafton. Much of the way, the road winds through wooded country with the odd cleared meadow or stone wall announcing the next farm.

Grafton Village Cheese Company

Just as Route 121 drops you into Grafton Village, take your first right onto Townshend Road. The cheese factory is about a mile down on the left.

Built to fit with the community's historic white clapboard buildings, the Grafton Village Cheese factory sits unobtrusively a short distance from the village center. The factory turns out significant quantities of cheddar (about 1.5 million pounds a year) but manages to keep its product high quality. In fact, factory officials recently decided not to expand to meet growing demand for their aged cheddar for fear the change would affect quality.

While at the factory, you can watch the cheese being made or pick some up at the gift shop. There you will find the full array of Grafton cheeses, which include cheddars of varying sharpness, as well as flavored versions, such as maple smoked, sage, and garlic. The store also sells maple syrup, other Vermont food products, and even hats and t-shirts bearing the Grafton logo.

✦ Westminster to Dummerston

From Grafton we will head south toward the superb apple-growing country of southeastern Vermont. Along the way, we'll stop at an organic dairy farm.

From Grafton Village take Route 121/35 East out of Grafton. At

Cambridgeport you'll continue east on Route 121. As you are entering the village of Saxtons River, turn right onto Westminster West Road. The road will roll and wind out of Saxtons River, and then the land will begin to open up. Eight miles south of Saxtons River, you'll see Livewater Farm on your right.

Livewater Farm

Bill and Muffin Acquaviva moved here about a decade ago to run their certified organic dairy farm. The farm itself dates back to about the 1930s. This is strictly a working farm, so the Acquavivas don't offer tours of the property. They do, however, have a small retail shop where they sell foods they make on the premises, including their jams, jellies, pickles, maple products, and seasonal produce such as garlic. Someone is always working on the farm, so they will greet you when you drive up.

Dwight Miller and Son Orchards

If southeastern Vermont has been gaining a following recently for its cheese, it has a much older reputation for being superb apple-growing country. Parts of the area are quite temperate compared to the rest of the state. Some people call it, only half jokingly, part of "Vermont's banana belt." That belt lies across the land that Read Miller farms.

To reach the Millers' orchards, continue down Westminster West Road. Five miles after leaving Livewater Farm you will reach Putney, where you will meet Route 5. Turn right and follow the road south. Three miles down on the right, you will see School House Road on your right. Turn here. After 1 mile, you will turn right onto Miller Road. You will soon pass part of the orchards on your right. The farm buildings are just ahead on your left.

Read and his wife, Malah, run Dwight Miller and Son Orchards (Read is actually the son). The Miller family is not exactly new to the area. The road the orchard sits on is named after the family. In fact, the family owned the land long before that road was created.

Their original title was issued by the Massachusetts Bay Colony, long before Vermont was a state.

Miller Orchards is one of those incredibly diverse agricultural businesses. The farm had the first registered Holsteins in the state and is perhaps Vermont's longest continuously operating maple sugar operation. The Millers grow 45 varieties of apples and 25 varieties of peaches. They also cultivate pears and all manner of berries, press their own cider, brew their own root beer, make an array of pickles and jellies, and grow tomatoes and salad greens in their greenhouses. And that is just a partial list. They sell what they make to large grocery stores, smaller food stores, at the Brattleboro Farmers' Market, and at their farmstand.

But Miller downplays the size of the operation, emphasizing that the farm is more significant for its history and for the fact that they grow everything organically. By the way, Miller says the banana belt ends on his property. He swears that in one stretch of his property peaches grow just fine, but that just across the road they won't.

Scott Farm

Just another couple miles away is another of the region's best-known orchards, Scott Farm. To get there, return on Miller Road to School House Road, and turn left. Then take your first right onto Eastwest

An Apple a Day

The Vermont Apples Web site (www.vermontapples.org) offers the following Vermont apple facts:

- Vermont's fresh apple crop is valued at $10–12 million a year. Processed apple products, like cider, applesauce, and hard cider bring an additional $10–12 million into the state annually.
- Vermont's leading apple varieties are McIntosh, Cortland, Red Delicious, and Empire.
- McIntosh apples became the state's leading variety after an extremely cold winter (1917–1918) devastated most other varieties.
- The Vermont legislature has designated the apple as the state fruit, and the apple pie as the state pie.

Road and almost immediately take another right onto Tucker Reed Road. Follow this road for 1 mile, until it dead-ends at Houghton Road. Turn right, then take your first left onto Kipling Road (named after the author, who owned a house in town). In another mile, you'll be at the Scott Farm.

Although it doesn't date back as far as Miller Orchards, the Scott Farm has a proud history of its own. The farm was started in 1862 and was on the cutting edge when it began shipping apples and maple syrup in the early 1900s.

Today the 560-acre farm is still wedded to the past in many ways. Orchardist Ezekiel Goodband oversees the growing of 70 kinds of apples, many of them heirloom varieties, as well as peaches, plums, European and Asian pears, wine and table grapes, cherries, medlars, quince, grapes, raspberries, nectarines, blueberries, and elderberries. You'll find many of these fruits at the self-service farmstand, which is open from August through Thanksgiving. The farm also offers pick-your-own apples and berries in season.

Part of the farm's mission is to educate, so staff here offer tours of the facilities, as well as tasting sessions of heirloom apples and fruit. The staff also conduct classes on such subjects as grafting, pruning, and backyard fruit growing.

Owned by the Landmark Trust, a nonprofit organization that recently inherited the property from its long-time owner, the farm features many historic white barns and a farmhouse that stands among them. Landmark Trust is restoring some buildings on the site and converting them for overnight rental, so you can wake up in the morning and take in the view of Vermont's banana belt.

If you want to return to Brattleboro after visiting the Scott Farm, follow Kipling Road for 2 miles, until it takes you to Route 5 again. Turn right onto Route 5 and continue for about 3 miles into town.

Details

Robb Family Farm and Country Shop
Brattleboro
888-318-9087
www.robbfamilyfarm.com
　　Open from 10 a.m. to 5 p.m. every day, except Wednesday; Sunday from 1 to 5 p.m.

Adams Farm
Wilmington
802-464-3762
www.adamsfamilyfarm.com
　　The farm grounds are open Wednesday through Sunday from 10 a.m. to 5 p.m. To explore the grounds and barn (allow two to three hours) you must purchase a Farm Experience Pass. Check the Web site or call for current rates. The store features the farm's own goats' milk soap, maple syrup, yarns, and wools, as well as locally made quilts, cheeses, and other Vermont specialty foods. Open daily from 10 a.m. to 5 p.m.

Olallie Daylily Gardens
South Newfane
802-348-6614
www.daylilygarden.com
　　The gardens officially open on June 1, and hours are Thursday through Sunday, 10 a.m. to 5 p.m. During peak season (mid-July to mid-August) the gardens are open daily. The gardens return to the Thursday-through-Sunday schedule from mid-August until Labor Day, when they close for the season. If you are visiting when the gardens would ordinarily be closed, you can call to set up an appointment.

Dutton Farm Stand
Newfane
802-365-4168
www.duttonberryfarm.com
　　Open every day but Christmas, 9 a.m. to 7 p.m.

Peaked Mountain Farm
Townshend
802-365-4502
pkmtfarm@sover.net
www.vtcheese.com/vtcheese/peaked/peaked.html
　　Cheese is made four days a week from May through October, but the schedule varies. Visitors are welcome any day of the week.

Taylor Farm
Londonderry
802-824-5690
www.taylorfarmvermont.com
www.vtcheese.com/vtcheese/trail/
Taylor/taylor.html

Open daily. Cheese is made
two or three days a week. The
afternoon milking happens at
4:30 p.m. In winter, sleigh rides
are offered hourly between 11
a.m. and 7 p.m. Along the way,
there is a stop for hot apple cider
and marshmallows.

Grafton Village
Cheese Company
Grafton
800-472-3866
www.graftonvillagecheese.com
www.vtcheese.com/vtcheese/trail/
Grafton/grafton.html

The retail store at the factory
is open Monday through Friday
from 8 a.m. to 4:30 p.m.;
weekends from 10 a.m. to 4 p.m.

Livewater Farm
Westminster West
802-387-4412
Open daily from 9 a.m. to 6 p.m.

Dwight Miller Orchards
Dummerston
802-254-9158

Open daily from 9 a.m. to 5
p.m. Farm tours are available for

larger groups, call ahead to make
arrangements. If you want to learn
about organic apple growing, call
ahead to make sure Read Miller
will be available to talk.

Scott Farm
Dummerston
802-254-6868
www.landmarktrustusa.org (click
on the Scott Farm link)

The self-service farm stand is
open daily during daylight hours
between August and Thanksgiving. Pick-your-own berry season
begins in late May and early June.
Early apple varieties ripen
beginning in July. The farm hosts
occasional tastings of sparkling
wines made from the orchard's
apples by Putney Mountain
Winery. Each fall, the farm hosts
an heirloom apple day. Check the
Web site or call for details.

Restaurants

Riverview Café
Brattleboro
802-254-9841
www.riverviewcafe.com

The café, which has a
sweeping view of the Connecticut
River, serves lunch (or Sunday
brunch) and dinner every day.
Lunch options, including salads,

soups, sandwiches, seafood platters, and the like, range from about $6 to $11. Dinner offerings—everything from tacos and seafood to steak and chicken—cost between $12 and $20.

Windham Hill Inn
800-944-4080
www.windhamhill.com

Dinner is served nightly in the elegant, candlelit restaurant, known for its extensive wine list. The menu changes seasonally to feature the freshest available ingredients. Entrées range in price from $25 to $29. Dinner dress is "smart casual." Jackets are not required for men, but are appropriate. Reservations recommended.

Lodging

Old Tavern at Grafton
Grafton
800-843-1801
www.windham-foundation.org/oldtavern

The Old Tavern has 11 rooms in the main building and offers an additional 19 in nearby cottages. The tavern also has four guest houses, which sleep 6 to 10 people. Room rates run from $135 to $390, depending on size

and season. Rates include a full breakfast.

Landmark Trust, USA
Dummerston
www.landmarktrustusa.org
802-254-6868

The Landmark Trust, USA, is a nonprofit historic preservation organization that rents its restored properties by the night. Prices vary by season. In southern Vermont, the group has converted a former maple sugarhouse on the Scott Farm in Dummerston into a small guest house, which can be rented for $100–$130 per night. Also on the Scott Farm is the Dutton Farmhouse. This is the most recent renovation, so check the Web site or call for rates. Just up the road from the farm is the home author Rudyard Kipling owned while living in Vermont. It rents for between $165 and $430 per night. Finally, the Landmark Trust rents the Amos Brown House in Whitingham, which sleeps six, for $165 to $230 per night.

For more lodging options, check the extensive listings at www.vermontvacation.com or call 800-VERMONT.

RESOURCES

Vermont Farms

Here are some additional farms you can visit, taken from the membership of Vermont Farms!, an organization of farms that welcome visitors. For further information, visit their Web site at www.vermontfarms.org (Note: This list does not repeat Vermont Farms! members that are part of the tours in the book.)

Northern Vermont

Adams Apple Orchard and Farm Market
1168 Old Stage Road
Williston VT 05495
802-879-5226; Toll-free
888-387-4288
www.upickvermont.com

Arcana Gardens & Greenhouses
175 Schillhammer Road
Jericho, VT 05465
802-899-5123
www.arcana.ws

Bonnieview Farm
2228 South Albany Road
Craftsbury Common,
VT 05827
802-755-6878

Couture's Maple Shop & Farmstay
560 Vt. Rt. 100
Westfield, VT 05874
802-744-2733;
800-845-2733 outside Vt.
www.maplesyrupvermont.com

Grand Isle Nursery and Garden Center
50 Ferry Road
South Hero, VT 05486
802-372-8805
www.grandislenursery.com

Miller's Family Farm
2378 Vt. Rte. 109
Waterville, VT 05492
802-644-5007;
802-644-5500;
888-302-FARM

Northern Vermont Llama Company & Choose and Cut Christmas Trees
766 Lapland Rd.
Waterville, VT 05492
802- 644-2257

Orrgle Hill Farm
386 Old Stage Road
Essex Junction VT 05452
802-879-5469
www.orrglehillfarm.com

The Parent Farmhouse
854 Pattee Hill Road
Georgia, VT 05468
802-524-4201

Rooster Ridge Farm Bed and Breakfast
114 Marsh Road
Wolcott, VT 05680
802-472-8566
www.vtlink.net/users/rooster

Central Vermont

Champlain Valley Alpacas and Farmstay
326 Fiddler's Lane
Bridport, VT 05734
802-758-FARM 3276
www.wcvt.com/~alpaca

Goodrich's Maple Farm
2427 U.S. Rte. 2
Cabot, VT 05647
Toll-free 800-639-1854 or
802- 426-3388
www.goodrichmaplefarm.com

Maple Ridge Sheep Farm
1187 Connecticut Corners Road
Randolph, VT 05060
802-728-3081
www.mrsf.com

Mountain Valley Farm
1719 Common Road
Waitsfield, VT 05673
802-496-9255
www.mountainvalleyfarm.com

Nebraska Knoll Sugar Farm
Lew and Audrey Coty
256 Falls Brook Lane
Stowe, VT 05672
802-253-4655

New England Maple Museum
U.S. Rte. 7
Rutland, VT 05701
802-483-9414

Redrock Farm
Two Redrock Lane
Chelsea, VT 05039-9039
802-685-4343;
866-685-4343
www.christmastrees.net

Round Barn Merinos
4263 Rte. 7
Ferrisburgh, VT 05456
802-877-6544

Round Robin Farm/ Marge's B&B
RR 1 Box 52
Sharon, VT 05065
802-763-7025

Snowshoe Farm
520 The Great Road
Peacham, VT 05862
802-592-3153
www.alpacas-
snowshoefarm.com

Sugar And Spice
Route 4
Mendon, VT 05701
802-773-7832

**Swenson Farm
Sawyer Mountain
Snowshoe Trails**
2765 Rt. 5 N
Fairlee, VT 05045
802-333-4137
www.vtsnowshoetrails.
com

**Yankee Kingdom
Orchard**
2769 Lake Street
W. Addison, VT 05491
802-759-2387
www.yankeekingdom
orchard.com

Southern Vermont

Andover Farms
2801 North Hill Road
Andover, VT 05143
802-875-2758

**Baked Apples at
Shearer Hill Farm
Bed & Breakfast**
Shearer Hill Road
Mount Snow Valley
Wilmington, VT 05363
802-464-3253;
800-437-3104
www.shearerhillfarm.com

Cas-Cad-Nac Farm
551 Wheeler Camp Rd.
Perkinsville, VT 05151
802-263-5740
www.cas-cad-nacfarm.com

**Christmas Trees of
Vermont and Farm Stay**
456 Old Connecticut
River Rd.
Springfield, VT 05156
Toll Free 877 817-0810
or 802- 885-2088
www.christmastrees
vermont.com

**D & Ks Butterfly Heaven
and Garden Center**
3417 Vt. Rte. 30
Jamaica, VT 05343
802-874-4160
www.butterfliesandbirds
invermont.com

Elysian Hills Tree Farm
209 Knapp Rd.
Dummerston, VT 0530
802-257-0233
www.elysianhillsfarm.
com

**Green Mountain
Orchards**
130 West Hill Road
PO Box 225
Putney VT 05346
802-387-5851
www.greenmountain
orchards.com

Harlow's Sugar House
563 Bellows Falls Rd.
Putney, VT 05346
802-387-5852
www.harlowssugarhouse.
com

Mountain Pond Farm
74 Obed Moore Rd.
Weston, VT 05161
802-824-8190

North River Winery
201 Vt. Rte. 112
Jacksonville, VT 05342
802-368-7557
www.northriverwinery.
com

**Taylor Farm
and Guesthouse**
825 Route 11
Londonderry, VT 05148
802-824-5690
www.vtcheese.com/
taylor.htm

Wellwood Orchard
529 Wellwood
Orchard Rd.
Springfield VT 05156
802-263-5200

West Mountain Farm
240 Maltese Rd.
Stamford, VT 05352
802-694-1417

Vermont Fresh Network

Here are some additional restaurants that feature Vermont-grown and produced food on their menus. All are members of the Vermont Fresh Network, an organization that encourages farmers, food producers, and chefs to work directly with each other. For further information, visit their Web site at www.vermontfresh.net (Note: This list does not repeat Vermont Fresh Network members that are mentioned elsewhere in the book.)

Northwestern Vermont

158 Main
158 Main St.
Jeffersonville, VT 05464
802-644-8100

Alburg Country Club
230 Route 129
Alburg, VT 05440
802-796-3586

Alex's VT Soup Company
1636 Williston Rd.
South Burlington, VT 05403
802-862-5678

Bailey's at the Valley
4302 Bolton Access Rd.
Bolton Valley, VT 05477
802-434-3444

Bee's Knees
82 Lower Main St.
Morrisville, VT 05661
802-888-7889

Black Lantern
2057 North Main St.
Route 118
Montgomery, VT 05470
802-326-4507

Brass Lantern Inn B & B
717 Maple St.
Stowe, VT 05672
802-253-2229

Café Piccolo
431 Pine St.
Burlington, VT 05401
802-862-5515

Café Shelburne
Shelburne Rd.
Shelburne, VT 05482
802-985-3939

Cannon's Italian Restaurant
1127 North Ave.
Burlington, VT 05401
802-652-5151

Chow Bella
28 N. Main St.
St. Albans, VT 05478
802-524-1405

Five Spice Café
175 Church St.
Burlington, VT 05401
802-864-4045

Foothills Bakery
1123 Main Street
Fairfax, VT
802-849-6601

Gables Inn
1457 Mountain Rd.
Stowe, VT 05672
802-253-7730

Greenstreets Restaurant
30 Main St.
Burlington, VT 05401
802-862-4930

Inn at Shelburne Farms
1611 Harbor Rd.
Shelburne, VT 05482
802-985-8498

Kitchen Table Bistro
1840 West Main St.
Richmond, VT 05477
802-434-8686

Leunig's Bistro
115 Church St.
Burlington, VT 05401
802-863-3759

Mirabelle's
198 Main St.
Burlington, VT 05401
802-658-3074

Oasis Diner
189 Bank St.
Burlington, VT 05401
802-864-5308

Pauline's Café
1834 Shelburne Rd.
South Burlington, VT 05401
802-862-1081

Perry's Fish House
1080 Shelburne Rd.
South Burlington, VT 05403
802-862-1300

**Sirloin Saloon
of Shelburne**
Route 7
Shelburne, VT 05482
802-985-2200

Smokejacks Restaurant
156 Church St.
Burlington, VT 05401
802-658-1119

**Sneakers Bistro
and Café**
36 Main St.
Winooski, VT 05404
802-655-9081

**Stoweflake Mountain
Resort and Spa**
1746 Mountain Rd.
Stowe, VT 05672
802-253-7355

Sugarsnap
505 Riverside Ave.
Burlington, VT 05401
802-652-5922

Sweetwater's
120 Church St.
Burlington, VT 05401
802-864-9800

Timberholm Inn
452 Cottage Club Rd.
Stowe, VT 05672-4294
802-253-7603

**Topnotch at Stowe:
Maxwell's & Buttertub
Bistro**
4000 Mountain Rd.
Stowe, VT 05672
802-253-8585

Trattoria Delia
152 St. Paul St.
Burlington, VT 05401
802-864-5253

**Three Tomatoes Trattoria
Burlington**
83 Church St.
Burlington, VT 05401
802-660-9533

Northeastern Vermont

Highland Lodge
1290 Craftsbury Rd.
Greensboro, VT 05841
802-533-2647

Inn on the Common
1162 N. Craftsbury Rd.
Craftsbury Common, VT
05482
802-586-9619

**Lakeview Inn
& Restaurant**
295 Breezy Ave.
Greensboro, VT 05841
802-533-9816

**Loon's Landing
Restaurant & Sa-Loon**
135 Main St.
Box 191
Island Pond, VT 05846
802-723-5666

East-Central Vermont

1824 House Inn
2150 Main St.
Waitsfield, VT 05673
800-426-3986

**Alchemist Pub and
Brewery**
23 South Main St.
Waterbury, VT 05676
802-244-4120

Allechante
Main & Elm Streets
Norwich, VT 05055
802-649-1863

Bear Creek Mtn. Club
Route 100, 9 miles West
of Woodstock
Plymouth, VT 05056
802-672-4242

Birds Nest Inn
5088 Waterbury-Stowe
Rd.
Waterbury Center, VT
05677
802-244-7490

**Capitol Grounds Café
and Roastery**
45 State Street
Montpelier, VT 05602
802-223-7800

Carpenter & Main
326 Main St.
Norwich, VT 05055
802-649-2922

Castle
At the Junction of Routes
103 and 131
Proctorsville, VT 05149
802-226-7361

Coffee Corner
83 Main Street
Montpelier, VT
802-229-9060

**Common Man
Restaurant**
3209 German Flats Rd.
Warren, VT 05674
802-583-2800

**Harpoon Brewery Beer
Garden**
336 Ruth Carney Dr.
Windsor, VT 05089
802-674-5491

Hatchery
164 Main St.
Ludlow, VT 05149
802-228-2311

Inn at Idlewood
HCR 65
Box 17
Sharon, VT 05065
802-763-5236

Inn at the Round Barn
1661 East Warren Rd.
Waitsfield, VT 05673
802-583-1091

Inn at Weathersfield
1342 Route 106
Perkinsville, VT 05151
802-263-9217

Julio's Restaurant
54 State St.
Montpelier, VT 05602
802-229-9348

Kristina's Kitchen
30 North Main St.
Rochester, VT 05767
802-767-4258

La Pizzeria of Montpelier
23 Berlin St.
Montpelier, VT 05602
802-229-5122

Michael's on the Hill
4182 Stowe-Waterbury
Rd. Rte. 100
Waterbury Center, VT
05677
802-244-7476

Millbrook Inn
& Restaurant
533 Mill Brook Rd.
Waitsfield, VT 05673
802-496-2405

Mist Grill
92 Stowe St.
Waterbury, VT 05676
802-244-8522

October Country Inn
P.O. Box 66
Bridgewater Corners, VT
05035
802-672-3412

Perfect Pear Café
Main St.
Bradford, VT 05033
802-222-5912

Tanglewoods Restaurant
179 Guptil Rd.
Waterbury Center, VT
05677
802-244-7855

Three Stallion Inn
Stock Farm Rd.
Randolph, VT 05060
802-728-5575

Village Inn of Woodstock
41 Pleasant St.
Woodstock, VT 05091
802-457-1255

Woodstock Inn
and Resort
14 The Green
Woodstock, VT 05091
802-457-1100

West-Central
Vermont

American Flatbread
at the Marbleworks
137 Maple St.
Suite 29 F
Middlebury, VT 05753
802-388-3300

Back Home Again Café
23 Center St.
Rutland, VT 05701
802-775-9800

Basin Harbor Club
4800 Basin Harbor Rd.
Vergennes, VT 05491
802-475-2311

Birdseye Diner
590 Main St.
Castleton, VT 05735
802-468-2213

Choices Restaurant
140 Wobbly Lane
Killington, VT 05751
802-422-4030

Countryman's Pleasure
3 Townline Rd.
Mendon, VT 05071
802-773-7141

Eat Good Food
221 Main St.
Vergennes, VT 05491
802-877-2772

Green Peppers
Restaurant
10 Washington St.
Middlebury, VT 05753
802-388-9276

Hemingway's Restaurant
4988 US Route 4
between junctions 100N
and 100S
Killington, VT 05751
802-422-3886

Inn at Baldwin Creek and
Mary's Restaurant
1868 North Route 116
Bristol, VT 05443
802-453-2432

Lilac Inn
53 Park St.
Brandon, VT 05733
800-221-0720

**Mountain Top Inn
and Resort**
195 Mountain Top Rd.
Chittenden, VT 05737
802-83-2311

Red Clover Inn
Woodward Rd.
Mendon, VT 05701
800-752-0571

**Roland's Place/
1796 House**
3629 Ethan Allen
Highway
New Haven, VT 05472
802-453-6309

Sirloin Saloon of Rutland
Route 7
Rutland, VT 05701
802-773-7900

Starry Night Café
5371 Rte. 7
Ferrisburgh, VT 05456
802-877-6316

Swift House Inn
25 Stewart Lane
Middlebury, VT 05753
802-388-9925

Waybury Inn
457 East Main St.
East Middlebury, VT
05740
802-388-4015

Whitford House
912 Grandey Rd.
Vergennes, VT 05491
802-758-2704

Southern Vermont

Deerhill Inn
14 Valley View Rd.
West Dover, VT 05356
802-464-3100

Dorset Inn
On the Green
Dorset, VT 05251
802-867-5500

Four Columns Inn
On the Green
Newfane, VT 05345
802-365-7713

Inn at West View Farm
2928 Route 30
Dorset, VT 05251
802-867-5715

Izabella's Eatery
351 West Main St.
Bennington, VT 05201
802-447-4949

Nutmeg Country Inn
153 Rt 9 West
Wilmington, VT 05363
802-464-7400

Putney Inn
57 Putney Landing Rd.
Putney, VT 05346
802-387-5517

**Sirloin Saloon
of Manchester**
Routes 11 & 30
Manchester, VT 05255
802-362-2600

Spiral Press Café
15 Bonnet St.
Manchester Center, VT
05255
802-362-5465

Three Mountain Inn
Route 30
Jamaica, VT 05343
802-874-4140

Ye Olde Tavern
5183 Main St.
Manchester, VT 05255
802-362-0611

INDEX